2x4

FURNITURE

2x4
FURNITURE

Simple, Inexpensive & Great-Looking Projects You Can Make

STEVIE HENDERSON

A Sterling/Lark Book
Sterling Publishing Co., Inc.   New York

To my husband, Jim

Editor: Leslie Dierks
Design: Alex Alford
Illustrations: Jay S. Kelly
Photography: Evan Bracken
Photo Assistance: Preston Poe
Production: Elaine Thompson, Alex Alford
Project Design and Assistance: Mark Baldwin

Library of Congress Cataloging-in-Publication Data

Henderson, Stevie [date]
   2x4 furniture : simple, inexpensive & great-looking projects
you can make / Stevie Henderson.
     p.   cm.
   "Sterling/Lark book."
   Includes index.
   ISBN 0-8069-0293-0
   1. Furniture making.   I. Title.   II. Title: Two by four furniture.
TT194.H46 1992
684.1'042—dc20   92–21529
                                          CIP

10 9 8 7 6 5 4 3

A Sterling/Lark Book

First paperback edition published in 1994 by
Sterling Publishing Company, Inc.
387 Park Avenue South, New York, N.Y. 10016

Produced by Altamont Press, Inc.
50 College Street, Asheville, NC 28801

© 1993 by Stevie Henderson

Distributed in Canada by Sterling Publishing
  % Canadian Manda Group, P.O. Box 920, Station U©
  Toronto, Ontario, Canada M8Z 5P9
Distributed in Great Britain and Europe by Cassell PLC
  Villiers House, 41/47 Strand, London WC2N 5JE, England
Distributed in Australia by Capricorn Link Ltd.
  P.O. Box 665, Lane Cove, NSW 2066

Sterling ISBN 0-8069-0293-0 Trade
               0-8069-0294-9 Paper

CONTENTS

INTRODUCTION

The furniture pieces chosen for this book were designed to be practical, easy to make, economical, and sturdy. They all use dimensional lumber and basic hardware available in any local home center, and all can be made with simple hand tools. You need not be an engineering genius or a master craftsperson to build the stylish furniture contained in this book. The plans for each project include a description of the materials required, a cutting list of all of the component parts, step-by-step instructions, and assembly drawings. These will all help you to produce finished products that you will want to show off to your neighbors.

The construction techniques are chosen for their simplicity and ease. As a general rule, the joints are uncomplicated—secured with nails and screws—rather than the more complex ones required in advanced woodworking books. This will undoubtedly disappoint those of you who want to make lapped goose-necked mortise-and-tenon joints with stub tenons. On the other hand, it will probably come as a great relief to those who simply wish to build sturdy, handsome furnishings in a time-efficient manner. Of course, those of you who wish to alter the construction and include halved rabbetted oblique scarf joints, will no doubt know where to substitute them.

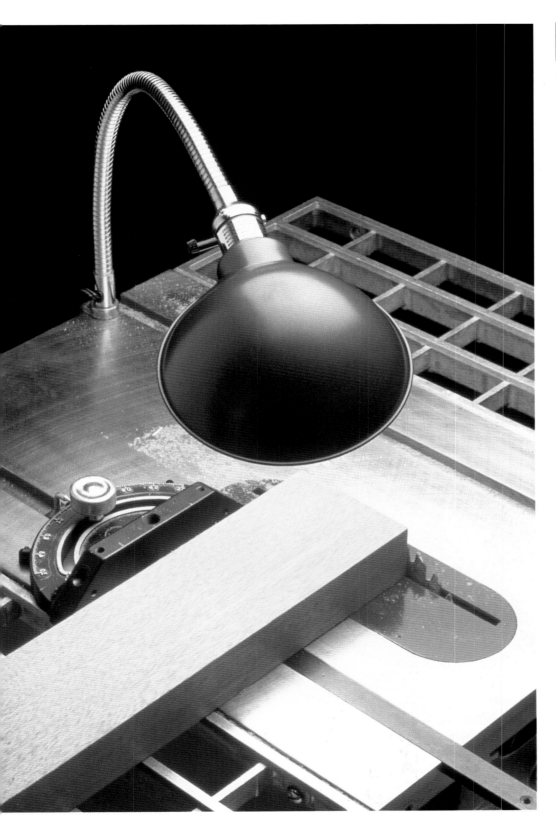

TIPS & TECHNIQUES

No matter whether you are a beginner or an experienced woodworker, even your very first woodworking project can be better than most manufactured pieces. Just take your time and exercise some patience. I don't claim to be a master craftsperson, but I like working with wood and am very pleased with the projects that I have created for my home. Not only is woodworking a soothing and therapeutic pastime, but it certainly is cheaper to make your own furniture—and you can build it to your own specifications.

As with any other activity, selecting quality materials and using good tools will produce a better-looking finished project, and make it easier to construct.

LUMBER

While on the surface (no pun intended) it would seem that one board is pretty much like any other, in actuality there are many differences in wood. Being aware of these differences will enable you to choose the right wood for your project.

Wood is classified as either hardwood or softwood. Hardwood comes from deciduous trees such as maple, cherry, and walnut, which shed their leaves every year. Softwood is cut from coniferous trees (evergreens) such as pine, redwood, and cedar.

Each tree has its own unique qualities, including different grain patterns and fiber density. Cedar has a distinctive odor that repels moths, and redwood is insect resistant. In addition, other woods may be chemically treated, which makes them suitable for exterior use.

As the classification implies, softwood is easier to cut, drill, and nail or screw into than is hardwood. It is also much less expensive, so it is a good choice for a beginning woodworker.

Softwood is sold in standard dimensional sizes such as 2 x 4 and 1 x 12, and in specific lengths such as 6 feet, 8 feet, and 10 feet. Therefore, the bin labeled 2 x 4 x 8 at your local building-supply store contains 2 x 4 boards that are 8 feet long.

While it might appear that this makes it easy (a 2 x 4 should be 2 inches thick and 4 inches wide, right?), this is not the case. Apparently the lumber manufacturers have conspired to drive us all crazy. The rough board was 2 inches by 4 inches before it was planed to a smooth surface on all four sides. After surfacing, a 2 x 4 actually measures 1-1/2 inches by 3-1/2 inches. The chart below shows the nominal sizes (what the board is called) and the actual measurements of dimensional lumber.

Nominal Size	Actual Dimensions
1 x 2	3/4" x 1-1/2"
1 x 4	3/4" x 3-1/2"
1 x 6	3/4" x 5-1/2"
1 x 8	3/4" x 7-1/4"
1 x 10	3/4" x 9-1/4"
1 x 12	3/4" x 11-1/4"
2 x 2	1-1/2" x 1-1/2"
2 x 4	1-1/2" x 3-1/2"
2 x 6	1-1/2" x 5-1/2"
2 x 8	1/1-2" x 7-1/4"
2 x 10	1-1/2" x 9-1/4"
2 x 12	1-1/2" x 11-1/4"
4 x 4	3-1/2" x 3-1/2"
4 x 6	3-1/2" x 5-1/2"
6 x 6	5-1/2" x 5-1/2"
8 x 8	7-1/2" x 7-1/2"

To make matters worse, individual boards of the same nominal size may not always have precisely the same actual width—even if purchased at the same store at the same time. A difference of only 1/16 or 1/32 inch can mean that your project will not fit together correctly. Take the time to be safe; carefully check the wood that you buy.

Softwood is graded for its overall quality, which relates directly to price. "Select" wood is a better grade than "common," and therefore costs more. If you are building a rustic, outdoor project, then a lesser-quality wood will look fine. If you are building a coffee table to display in your living room, you'll want the better material. The softwood grades are listed below.

Common Grades:

No. 1 common - Contains small knots and a few imperfections, but should have no knotholes.

No. 2 common - Free of knotholes, but contains some knots.

No. 3 common - Contains larger knots and small knotholes.

No. 4 common - Used for construction only. Contains large knotholes.

No. 5 common - Lowest grade of lumber. Used only when strength and appearance are not necessary.

Select Grades:

B and better - (or 1 and 2 clear) - The best and most expensive grades used for the finest furniture projects.

C select - May have a few small blemishes.

D select - The lowest quality of the better board grades. It has imperfections that can be concealed with paint.

The clear boards (those that are nearly free of imperfections) come from the outer section of the tree. The center section (heartwood) contains more knots and other flaws.

All of the projects in this book may also be built with hardwood. It will take some calculating on your part, however, since hardwood is normally sold in random widths and lengths. Each board is cut from the log as wide and as long as possible. Consequently, hardwood is sold by a measure called the board foot. A board foot represents a piece of lumber 1 inch (or less) thick, 12 inches wide, and 1 foot long. Hardwood thicknesses are measured in quarter inches. The standard thicknesses are 3/4, 4/4, 5/4, 6/4, and 8/4. The board-foot measurement is doubled for boards thicker than one inch.

As you might guess, plywood is made from several plies of wood that are glued together. It is sold in sheets measuring 4 feet by 8 feet. In some supply stores you can also purchase half-sheets measuring 4 feet by 4 feet. Plywood comes in standard thicknesses of 1/8, 1/4, 3/8, 1/2, 5/8, and 3/4 inch.

There are two principal kinds of plywood: veneer-core and lumber-core. Lumber-core plywood is the higher quality material; its edges can be worked as you would work solid wood. The edges of veneer-core plywood must be either filled or covered because they are not attractive.

Plywood is also graded according to the quality of the outer veneer. The grades are "A" through "D," with "A" representing the best quality. A piece of plywood has two designations, one for each face. For example, an "A-D" piece has one veneered surface that is "A" quality and one that is "D" quality.

If plywood is designated "exterior" it means that the glue between the plies is waterproof. Interior-grade plywood should not be used where there is a lot of moisture.

While it is nice to know all of this information about wood and plywood, your own eyes will be the best test. It is tedious to carefully select boards in the store, but it will prevent much frustration later. Check each and every board that you buy for the following characteristics:

Knots and knotholes: Small, tight knots are acceptable, especially if you intend to paint the finished project. Large knotholes should be avoided. It is sometimes possible to cut your pieces to eliminate the knotholes, but you need to buy extra material to allow for the waste.

Warping and bowing: Wood has a tendency to warp or bow if it is not dried correctly. A warped board can be straightened, but it takes time and effort. It is easier to buy wood that is already in good condition.

Splitting: Avoid boards that are split on the ends or elsewhere in the wood, since the splits tend to continue (much like a run in a nylon stocking). If it is a very short split, you can simply cut off the split portion, but be sure to allow for the waste.

When you do the actual cutting of individual pieces, you should re-inspect each board. For example, if you have an 8-foot board and you need a 7-1/2-foot piece, look to see if there is a knot on either end. If so, eliminate the six inches with the knot in it. If the piece you are cutting or assembling has an outside and an inside, choose the better-looking surface for the outside. It will save you time later during the filling and sanding procedures, and give you a more attractive project.

For purposes of clarity, this book designates a name for each surface of a board. The broadest part of a board is called a face, and the narrow surface along the length of a board is an edge. The ends, as the name suggests, are the smallest surfaces occurring on the extremities of each board. (See *Figure 1*.)

The materials lists in this book are all specified in linear feet, which indicates only the total length you need. If the materials list indicates that you need 17 linear feet of 2 x 4 pine, you have several choices when you buy the necessary lumber. For example, you could buy one 2 x 4 that is 10 feet long and another that is 8 feet long, or you could buy one 12-foot-long 2 x 4 plus one that is 6 feet long. Your actual purchase should be based on three factors.

First, take a look at the cutting list for the project you intend to make. You certainly do not want to buy all of your 2 x 4s in 6-foot lengths if your project calls for a piece that is 7-1/2 feet long. In fact, it is always a good idea to read through the instructions completely before you shop for the materials. Then, if you are presented with a dilemma in the shopping process, you'll be able to make an educated choice.

Secondly, consider the type of finish that you want to apply to the completed project. If you plan to paint, you can purchase a lower grade of wood, since many imperfections can be covered with wood filler and paint. If you plan to stain the finished piece, pay particular attention to the grain of the wood that

you are buying, and choose boards that have a similar grain.

Thirdly, when you get to the store, inspect the various lengths of wood available. Sometimes the 6-foot 2 x 4s are knotted or warped, but the 12-foot lengths are nearly perfect. Then it makes sense to buy the same number of feet in longer boards.

It also makes sense to overbuy on materials. It is very frustrating to have to return to the store to buy just one more 2 x 4 because you miscut the last one that you had. Also bear in mind that the ends of boards are not necessarily square. You need to allow extra length so that you can square off the end of the board before you begin your measurements. I always add between 10 and 20 percent to the materials list to allow for waste and any cutting mistakes.

When you begin the actual cutting, start with the longest boards. If you miscut, you will still have plenty of material left to cut another piece and the miscut board can be used for the shorter pieces.

Figure 1

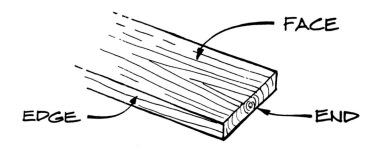

FACE

EDGE

END

MEASURING AND CUTTING

There is an old saying in woodworking: "Measure twice—cut once," and that is sound advice. The difference between having a project go together easily and experiencing absolute frustration is cutting the wood accurately.

As you would for any other task in woodworking, buy quality tools. A wide steel tape rule is a good choice for most projects. A narrow tape will bend more easily along the length of a board and will be less accurate. Consistently use the same measuring device throughout the project; unless you have precise measuring tools, any two instruments may vary enough to give you slightly different measurements.

Squares are versatile and essential tools in woodworking. The most commonly used types are the framing square (or carpenter's square) and the combination square. (See *Figure 2.*) In addition to their obvious use for marking a cutting line on a board and obtaining a right angle, squares can be used to check the outer or inner squareness of a joint, to guide a saw through a cut, and much more.

To measure certain pieces for your project, you may find that you need to enlarge a pattern from a scale drawing. If you are lucky enough to have access to a copy machine that you can set to exact percentages, it is a simple matter to enlarge the pattern until the scale is correct. Even if you do it by hand, enlarging a pattern is fairly easy.

Construct a grid of squares of the size specified in the scale drawing. For example, if the scale drawing indicates 1 square equals 1 inch, make your grid with 1-inch squares. Then transfer the design to your grid, working one square at a time.

When measuring and cutting, bear in mind that the saw blade has a thickness, and the same thickness (a kerf) will be removed from the wood by the blade. When you measure and mark a board, measure precisely. When you cut the board at your mark, set the saw so that the blade will exactly remove the mark. Cut so that you also remove the mark from the end of the board that will be waste.

Ripping (cutting along the length of a board) and crosscutting (cutting across the width of a board) are two of the most common ways of cutting wood. There is a specific tool for each, of course. A rip saw has

Figure 2

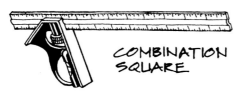

FRAMING SQUARE

COMBINATION SQUARE

teeth designed for cutting along the length of the board, with the grain, and a crosscut saw is made to cut across the grain.

While saw blades for power tools are also designed for ripping and crosscutting, the most practical blade for general woodworking is a combination blade. It rips and crosscuts with equal ease.

When you are cutting either lumber or plywood, note the type of cut that your tool is making, and use it to your advantage. For example, circular saws and saber saws cut on the upstroke, so they may leave ragged edges on the upper surface of your wood. When using these saws, you should position the wood with the better surface facing down when cutting.

Certain types of cuts, like hollowing out a section of wood, are done with chisels. Using a chisel well takes some practice, but it is worth the effort because chisels can perform unique woodworking tasks. Always work with sharp chisels. For your first purchase, choose a narrow chisel and one about an inch wide.

If you just need to "shave" a little off the end or along the edge of a board, a plane is the appropriate tool. Again, buy a sharp plane, and practice with it until you become fairly proficient.

MAKING JOINTS

There are many, many wood joints. They range in complexity from the plainest butt joint to lapped goose-necked mortise and tenon joints with stub tenons. The projects in this book are constructed with only the simplest joints, secured with either nails or screws.

Edge-to-edge joint: This joint is used when laminating boards together edge to edge to obtain a wider piece of wood. To ensure a perfect joint between boards, a minuscule amount should be ripped from each board. Next, wipe glue on the adjoining edges and clamp the boards together as shown in *Figure 3*.

Apply even pressure along the length of the piece. The boards should be firmly clamped, but not so tightly that all of the glue is forced out, or that the lamination starts to bow across its width. On a long lamination, extra boards may be placed above and below the lamination, across the width, and those boards clamped with "C" clamps or wood clamps. Wipe off any excess glue that is squeezed out in the clamping process.

Figure 3

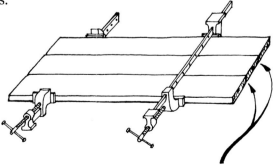

MAKING AN EDGE-TO-EDGE JOINT

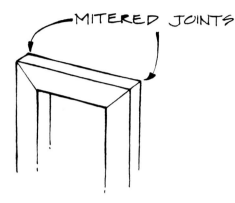

MITERED JOINTS

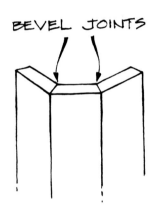

BEVEL JOINTS

Figure 4

Figure 5
Using Hand Tools to Make a Dado

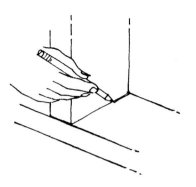

1. Mark the dimensions of the dado.

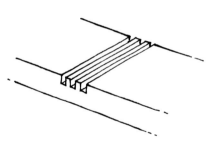

2. Cut to proper depth with saw.

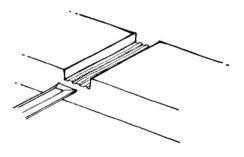

3. Chisel out excess (toward center).

Butt joint: This is the simplest of joints, where one board abuts another at a right angle. This method offers the least holding power of any joint. It must be reinforced with some kind of fastener, usually screws.

Miter: A miter is an angle cut across the width of a board. It is used to join two pieces of wood without exposing the end grain of either piece. A mitered joint must also be reinforced with nails or screws. The angle most often cut is 45 degrees, which is used to construct a right angle when two mitered boards are joined together.

Bevel: A bevel is also an angular cut, but it refers to an angle cut along the length of a board, rather than across the width as in a miter. *Figure 4* illustrates the difference between miters and bevels.

Dado: A dado is a groove cut in the face of one board to accommodate the thickness of another board. It can be cut with multiple saw passes, with a router, or with a dado set on a table saw. The procedure for making a dado using hand tools is shown in *Figure 5.*

No matter what kind of joint you're making, it is advisable to use both glue and fasteners (nails or screws) whenever possible. The only exception, when you may want to omit the glue, is on joints that you wish to disassemble at a later time.

ADHESIVES

For interior projects, ordinary, straw-colored carpenter's glue is the optimum choice. For exterior use, a two-part glue (resin plus a catalyst) works best.

Don't overdo the amount of glue. If you apply too much, the glue will be squeezed out and drip all over your project when the joint is clamped or fastened. I normally apply a small ribbon of glue down the center of one surface and then rub the adjoining surface against the ribbon to distribute the glue evenly. Your objective is to coat both surfaces with a uniform, thin coating.

When you mix a two-part adhesive, follow the manufacturer's directions explicitly. These glues set up very quickly, so only mix enough to perform the task at hand.

FASTENERS

Nails

Although there are many different types of nails (common, large flathead, duplex head, oval head, etc.), the one most commonly used in woodworking is a finishing nail. It has a much smaller head than the common nail, making it easy to recess below the surface of the wood (countersinking the nail). The small hole remaining on the surface is easily concealed with wood filler.

Nail sizes are designated by "penny" (abbreviated as "d"). Penny size directly corresponds to length,

although the diameter is larger for longer nails. They range in length from 1 inch to 6 inches. Some of the more commonly-used sizes of nails are listed in the table below.

Penny Size	Length (Inches)	Finishing Nails (Not to Scale)
2d	1	
3d	1-1/4	
4d	1-1/2	
5d	1-3/4	
6d	2	
7d	2-1/4	
8d	2-1/2	
9d	2-3/4	
10d	3	
12d	3-1/4	
16d	3-1/2	
20d	4	

As a general rule, when joining two pieces of wood together, use a nail length that will provide the greatest amount of holding power without penetrating the opposite surface. For example, if you are joining two 1 x 4s, each piece of wood is 3/4 inch thick—a total of 1-1/2 inches of wood. To maximize your holding power, you should choose a 1-1/4-inch-long nail.

Nails driven in at an angle provide more holding power than those that are driven straight into the work. Toenailing refers to the process of driving a nail into the wood at an extreme angle to secure two pieces together.

The most difficult part of toenailing comes when the nail is nearly into the wood and only the head and a bit of the shank are visible. To avoid making hammer marks on your wood, hammer the nail into the piece until the head is still slightly above the surface. Then use a nail set to finish the job and countersink the nail. (See *Figure 6*.)

In fact, the best way to prevent hammer marks on all of your work is to use a nail set. The trick to using a nail set effectively is to hold it in the proper manner. It should be steadied with the hand by gripping it firmly with all four fingers and your thumb. Rest your little finger on the surface of the wood for added stability.

If you are working with hardwood, a very narrow piece of softwood, or any wood that has a tendency to split when you nail into it, it is wise to pre-drill the nail hole. Choose a drill bit that is just barely smaller than the diameter of the nail, and drill a pilot hole about two-thirds the length of the nail.

If you are constructing a project that will be used out-of-doors, use only galvanized nails. When exposed to weather, ordinary nails will stain the

wood a black color, and ruin the appearance of your project.

Brads and Tacks
Wire brads are used for attaching trim or for very small projects. They are just a smaller and thinner version of finishing nails. They are designated in length in inches and wire gauge numbers from 11 to 20. The lower the gauge number, the larger the diameter.

Tacks have large heads and are used to attach fabric or other material to wood where light fastening is all that is required. The large-diameter head can be strictly ornamental or it can be used to hold something lightly in place.

Staples and Staple Guns
Staples are another light-duty fastener; they are often used to attach fabric to wood. A staple gun is a worthwhile investment and a handy piece of equipment to have around the house. Staple guns are available in many sizes and prices, and, although electric models are available, a heavy-duty hand staple gun will probably be all that you need initially. It is worthwhile to purchase staples in a variety of lengths to have them on hand to accommodate different materials.

Screws
The advantage of screws over nails is their holding power, and the fact that (when used without glue), they can be removed easily at a later date. Their disadvantage is that they are not as easy to insert.

Figure 6
Using a Nail Set

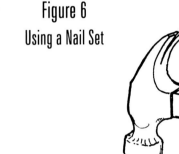
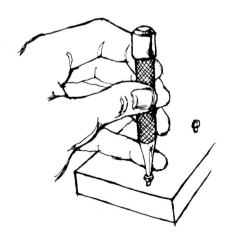

As with nails, there are many kinds of screws. The one most often used in woodworking is a flathead screw. As the name implies, it has a flat head that can be countersunk below the surface.

Screws are designated by length and diameter. In general, as with nails, you want to use the longest screw possible that won't penetrate the opposite surface. The diameter of a screw is described by its gauge number, as shown in *Figure 7*. Common sizes range from #2 to #16, with larger diameters having higher gauge numbers. You should use the largest diameter possible that does not risk splitting the wood.

When you are working on very soft wood it is possible to countersink a screw simply by driving it with a power drill. However, the resulting surface hole may only be covered by using wood filler. An alternate method is to pre-drill the screw hole and insert a wood plug over the top of the countersunk screw head.

This pre-drilling is normally a two-step operation. First drill the pilot hole using a drill bit the same diameter as the solid portion of the screw (minus the threads). Then drill the larger, countersink portion deep enough and at a diameter just slightly larger than the diameter of the screw head (or the depth and diameter to accommodate the screw and the wood plug you are

using). The larger diameter countersink portion of the drilling will center itself over the pilot hole. If you use the same size screws on a regular basis, you may wish to invest in a combination pilot-countersink bit for your drill, which will perform both operations at the same time.

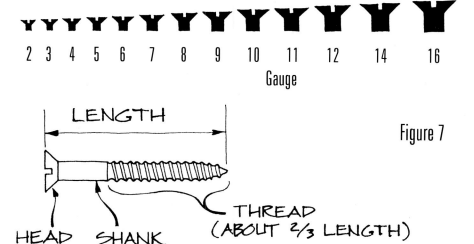

Gauge

Figure 7

LENGTH

HEAD   SHANK   THREAD (ABOUT ⅔ LENGTH)

You can purchase wood plugs, or you can cut your own. It is easy to slice a wooden dowel rod into many wood plugs. The only disadvantage to this plug is that it will show the end grain, and will be visible if you stain the wood. The alternative is to cut your own plugs using a plug cutter.

Screws can be inserted at an angle, the same way that nails are, to toe-nail two pieces of wood together. After some practice, you will be able to start a screw at an angle with little or no effort. If you find it difficult, simply use a drill or a screw starter to begin your screw hole.

One last note about screws—don't be stingy. My own rule of thumb is to join two pieces together; then apply some pressure to the joint to attempt to make it wobble. If it moves, I add some more screws. (Keep in mind that this advice comes from a modest-sized woman—I am sure that any football player could exert more pressure than I can.) You don't want to build a project that contains more weight from the metal screws than it does from the wood, but you also don't want to worry that it will come apart when you decide to move it into another room.

TOOLS

Woodworking tools are generally classified into three categories: hand tools (hammer, screwdriver, hand saw), portable power tools (circular saw, electric drill), and stationary power tools (table saw, band saw).

It is possible to build any project of wood using only hand tools—and many people do so. For them, much of the joy of woodworking is in the building process, and they are more concerned with the work itself than in how long it takes to complete it. Power tools are not necessary to produce quality results—they just work a lot faster. My enjoyment comes from seeing the finished project, and I prefer to expend the minimum amount of physical effort. Therefore, I use an electric drill rather than a screwdriver, and a table saw rather than a hand saw.

Buying Tools

If you are starting from scratch, buy the best tools that you can afford. This applies to everything—not just to stationary power tools. A poorly made hammer can be just as frustrating to use as a poorly made table saw.

When you are considering buying a new tool, a good source of information is the people who use it on a daily basis. Most woodworkers are happy to share their knowledge with you. If you don't know any carpenters, books and catalogs on woodworking tools are also good sources of information. Also check the warranty on a tool. If the manufacturer guarantees the tool for life, that's a good recommendation.

The projects in this book require some basic tools that, if you don't already own them, make useful additions to any household. Some tools, such as a saw and a set of screwdrivers, are needed for every project, but others, such as a staple gun, are only required for a few pieces. You may want to choose your first project according to the tools you have available; read through the instructions before starting a project to determine which tools you will need. All together, the tools required for all of these projects make a good starting set of woodworking equipment. They include the following:

Necessary (All Projects):

Working surface that is smooth and level
Measuring tools: tape measure, level, combination square
Hammers: two hammers (large and small), tack hammer, nail set
Screwdrivers: assortment of flat-head sizes
Saws: combination saw, or rip saw and cross-cut saw
Drill: hand or electric drill and a variety of bits
Clamps: two wood hand clamps, two "C" clamps
Sanding tools: sanding block and assortment of sandpaper from fine to coarse
Safety equipment: goggles, dust mask (use with power tools)

Optional (Some Projects Only):

Measuring tools: framing square
Clamps: web clamp, two bar clamps, two pipe clamps
Saws: saber saw (chisel can be used instead)
Chisels: 1/4-inch, 3/4-inch, and 1-inch wide

Not Necessary but Nice to Have:

Circular saw and selection of blades
Finishing sander
Router
Table saw
Band saw

Match the tool to your physical size and ability. A large man might like the performance and feel of a very large hammer. It would wear me out to lift it. I am more comfortable with a lighter hammer. I will probably have to hammer more times to drive in a nail, but it will be more suitable for me. The same philosophy applies to power tools. I once turned on a very large belt sander to sand a door. It was so powerful that it propelled me across the garage.

Some tools—hammers and saws are good examples—are universally recognized as being vital to working with wood. Others that are just as important are often ignored because their role is not as obvious. For me, having a solid work surface, a ready supply of clamps, and the right sanding equipment can spell the difference between enjoying my project and just muddling through it.

Working Surface

Probably the single most important tool in woodworking is a smooth and level work surface. It is virtually impossible to build a quality woodworking project without one. The range of work surfaces varies from the ridiculous to the sublime. It can be as simple as an old door (flush, not paneled) or a piece of plywood supported by sawhorses, or as elaborate as a professional-quality workbench costing thousands of dollars.

Bar clamps and pipe clamps come in a variety of sizes.

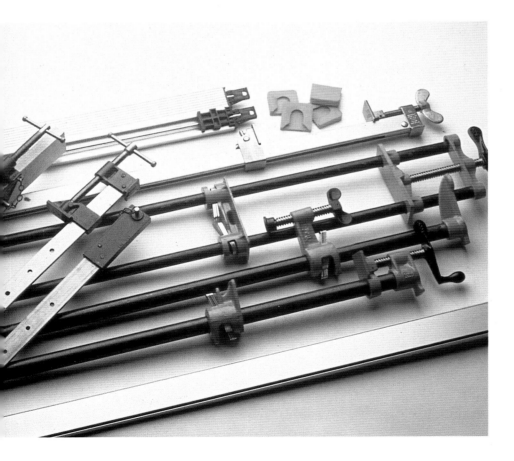

Whatever you use, make certain that it is large enough to accommodate the project you are building, that the surface is smooth and even, that it is solid enough to work on without shifting, and that it is perfectly level.

It is extremely simple to level any surface. Just set a fairly long level in various places on the surface, and turn the level so that it faces in several directions. If variations are noticed, shim the legs—or just underneath the work surface—with the thickness of wood that will raise the surface enough to be perfectly level. Attach the shim with glue and nails or screws to make certain that it stays in place while you work.

Clamps

A variety of clamps is absolutely necessary for woodworking. Not only are they used to hold joints together until the glue sets, but they are valuable aids when you try to assemble your project, a job that otherwise requires the concerted effort of several people. When you buy clamps, it is advisable to get two clamps of the same type. This is because you almost always use them in pairs to provide even pressure on the work.

When you apply clamps, always insert a piece of wood between the clamp and your work as a buffer. That way you will avoid leaving clamp marks on the surface.

Wood hand clamps are extremely versatile since they can be adjusted to clamp offset surfaces.

Bar clamps and pipe clamps can be used to hold assemblies together temporarily while you add the fasteners, as well as to apply pressure to laminates. While they look very much alike and function the same way, pipe clamps are significantly less expensive. You buy the fittings separately, and they can be used with various lengths of pipe, depending upon the need. You can also buy rubber "shoes" that fit over pipe clamp fittings, which will eliminate clamp marks on the wood.

"C" clamps are useful for many woodworking applications. They can hold two thicknesses of wood together, secure a piece of wood to a work surface, and perform many other functions. A "C" clamp can best be described as an extra helping hand.

Web clamps (or band clamps) are used for clamping such things as chairs or drawers, where a uniform pressure needs to be exerted completely around a project. It consists of a continuous band with an attached metal mechanism that can be ratcheted to pull the band tightly around the object.

Sanding

The amount of sanding that you do on each project depends in a large part on the intended use of the project, and on the what kind of finish you plan to use. Obviously, if you prefer a rustic look for your project, it need not be sanded completely smooth. However, a rustic chair requires more sanding than a rustic table—someone will be sitting on it. An indoor cabinet to be stained requires more sanding than one that will be painted.

Most sanding can be accomplished with power tools. A belt sander is often used for large jobs. It sands quickly, but it is difficult to control on softwood such as pine. Because of its power, a belt sander can easily gouge softwood or, if you don't watch carefully, it can remove more of the wood than you wish.

An orbital sander does a good job of beginning the sanding process, but it may leave circular marks that must be subsequently sanded out by hand.

A finishing sander is probably the most practical power sander for furniture projects. It has the ability to smooth the surface quickly, and it does not leave circular marks.

Put safety first, and wear the proper equipment to protect your eyes, ears, and lungs.

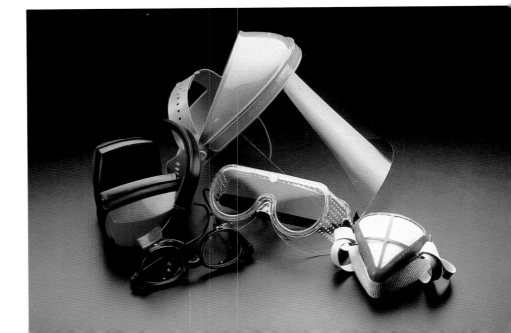

Of course, any project may be sanded by hand. To sand flat surfaces, wrap a block of wood with a piece of sandpaper. On moldings, use your hand or an object that conforms to the curve.

No matter what tool you use, begin sanding with a coarse grit and gradually progress to sandpaper with a fine grit.

FINISHES

All of the projects in this book are painted or stained, or a combination of both. One of the wonderful characteristics of wood is that you can apply an almost limitless variety of finishes to the same project. That means, if you like the design of a project, but would prefer it a bright purple, or stained very dark, you can "have it your way."

When you select a finish, keep in mind where the project will be used. I always use non-toxic finishes, but it is particularly important to choose substances that are not harmful if you are building something for use in a child's room. If your project will be used in the kitchen where it will be exposed to moisture, you probably should consider using a protective coat of polyurethane or spar varnish. All projects that will be used outside should be finished with an exterior-grade stain or paint, and sealed with a weather-proof sealer. Before using any product, read the directions carefully and follow them explicitly. It will save you lots of trouble.

Always use a sealer on raw wood before you paint. It seals the surface and prevents knotholes or other imperfections from weeping through your paint. In the long run, it will save time and materials too; sealing the wood will eliminate the need for multiple coats of paint.

Although there are professionals out there who will only use very expensive hog bristle brushes, I never buy any brush that must be cleaned. I have become addicted to sponge brushes, which can be thrown in the trash after use. Don't buy the ones that have visible holes on the surface like a kitchen sponge. Look for the ones that have a smooth surface like a cosmetic sponge. These brushes are very cheap (usually less than a dollar for even a 4-inch width).

One last hint on finishing: if you have to stop your painting or staining in the middle of the job, just pop your brush in an airtight sandwich bag. You can leave it there overnight, and it will not dry out.

SAFETY

Always bear in mind that working with power tools can be dangerous. I know many woodworkers, and some of them have missing digits. If that frightens you, that's good. It only takes one careless action to result in frightful consequences.

If you work with power tools, make sure that you know what you are doing. Read the instructions that come with the tools very carefully. Misuse of the equipment can lead to serious injury to yourself or damage to the tool.

Never take your eyes off of the work; always concentrate on what you are doing, and take the necessary safety precautions. Develop the habit of avoiding the path of the saw—do not stand directly behind it or directly in front of it. Power saws can flip a piece of wood back at you with incredible force.

It is always wise to wear some kind of safety goggles when working with wood. It only takes one splinter of wood flying toward your eye to make the purchase price and the practice of wearing goggles worth your while.

Because of the amount of sawdust that is produced when you work with wood, some sort of dust mask is a prudent accessory. Wood dust can be very irritating to your lungs. There are a number of different masks available, ranging from a simple paper mask to more sophisticated masks with replaceable filters.

Prolonged exposure to loud noise can have harmful effects on your hearing. If you use power tools for extended periods— especially power saws, which can be quite loud—a pair of ear plugs or protectors is a good investment.

Finally, just because you should be careful when working with wood doesn't mean that you can't enjoy yourself. As the project develops, take time out to savor the look, feel, and aroma of the freshly cut wood. Then, when you've finished, pat yourself on the back for a job well done. And don't be shy about showing off your accomplishment to your family and friends!

Metric Equivalency

INCHES	CM
1/8	0.3
1/4	0.6
3/8	1.0
1/2	1.3
5/8	1.6
3/4	1.9
7/8	2.2
1	2.5
1-1/4	3.2
1-3/4	4.4
2	5.1
2-1/2	6.4
3	7.6
3-1/2	8.9
4	10.2
4-1/2	11.4
5	12.7
6	15.2
7	17.8
8	20.3
9	22.9
10	25.4
11	27.9
12	30.5
13	33.0
14	35.6
15	38.1
16	40.6
17	43.2
18	45.7
19	48.3
20	50.8
21	53.3
22	55.9
23	58.4
24	61.0

Indoor Enjoyment

MATERIALS LIST

Lumber:

2 pcs. laminated pine (or oak), ea. 48" x 24"*
49 linear ft. 1 x 4 pine (or oak)*
15 linear ft. decorative molding, at least 3-1/2" wide
3 linear ft. 2 x 6 pine
4 table legs, each 14-1/2" long x 3-1/2" sq. at top*

Hardware:

approx. 100 #6 x 1-1/4" flathead wood screws
approx. 100 #6 x 2" flathead wood screws
approx. 50 #10 x 3" flathead wood screws

Special Tools and Techniques:

2 or 3 large bar clamps
saber saw or large chisel
miters

See "Notes on the Materials," below.

CUTTING LIST

Code	Description	Qty.	Material	Dimensions
A	Table Top	1	laminated pine (or oak)	46" sq.
B	Table Top Trim	4	1 x 4 pine (or oak), ripped	50" long
C	Leg	4	3-1/2" sq. newel post	14-1/2" long
D	Side Rail	4	1 x 4 pine	45-1/2" long
E	Corner Support	4	2 x 6 pine	5-1/2" x 5-1/2" x 7-3/4" (approx.)
F	Top Trim	4	1 x 4 pine	50" long
G	Side Trim	4	3-1/2" decorative molding	42" long

Notes on the Materials

The coffee table shown here is constructed from laminated 1 x 4 oak boards, but you can also use pine. Most building-supply stores sell sections of wood that have already been laminated. Of course, you can laminate the boards yourself, but I don't recommend it unless you are a very experienced woodworker and possess heavy-duty tools. Due to the number of boards and overall size, it is a bigger job than it looks. If you do laminate the boards yourself, the finished size of each of the two sections should be 23 by 46 inches.

For the legs, we can again circumvent the need for experienced woodworking skills. If you do not have a lathe (or don't want to turn your own legs), simply purchase

COFFEE TABLE

After looking through several decorating magazines and furniture store flyers, I decided that I simply could not live without a new, square coffee table in my living room. Unfortunately, the prices were too far out of reach and, obviously, the only solution was to build one myself. The finished table looks impressive, but never fear! The construction is simple, and it takes advantage of pre-made wood products that you can find at any large building-supply store.

four newel posts and cut them to length. Turned upside down, they make extremely attractive table legs—and who will guess?

Constructing the Table Top

1. If you purchased wood already laminated, trim all four sides of each of the two laminated sections to a finished size of 23 by 46 inches. This step ensures that the edges are square and provide a good bonding surface.

2. Place the two trimmed laminated sections, 46-inch sides together, on a level surface. Wipe glue on the meeting edges, and clamp them together securely with two or three bar clamps for at least 24 hours. The result is a table top (A) that now measures 46 inches square.

3. Cut four table top trim pieces (B) from 1 x 4 pine, each 50 inches long.

4. Rip each trim piece (B) to 2 inches in width. For assistance with ripping a piece of wood, refer to the "Tips and Techniques" section.

5. The next step is to frame the table top (A) with the 2-inch-wide trim pieces (B), as shown in *Figure 1*. First, setting each piece on its face, miter both ends of all four trim pieces (B) at a 45-degree angle. Then wipe glue on the mitered ends and meeting edges, and clamp the trim pieces (B) to the table top (A) using bar clamps. Leave the assembly undisturbed for at least 24 hours. The framed top now measures 50 inches square.

Constructing the Base

1. Cut each of the four newel posts to 14-1/2 inches long. These will be the legs (C). In order to support the side rails of the coffee table, we have to remove a corner section of wood from the square top of each of the four legs (C). This maneuver is designed to eliminate the need for making blind dadoes.

2. Set the depth of your saber saw to 1-3/4 inches. Make three cuts in the order shown in *Figure 2*. The blade edges in the drawing indicate the direction of the cuts. If you use a chisel instead, use the illustration to guide your cuts.

Cut and remove a rectangle of wood measuring 1-3/4 by 1-3/4 by 3-1/2 inches from the inside corner of each leg top as shown in *Figure 3*.

3. Cut four side rails (D) from the 1 x 4 pine, each 45-1/2 inches long. Setting each piece on its edge, miter both ends of each side rail (D) at a 45-degree angle, as shown in *Figure 4*.

4. This next step probably requires the assistance of a willing helper (or an unwilling helper and a baseball bat), and it should be performed on a level surface. Each of the legs (C) must be connected to the side rails (D), and the entire assembly must be perfectly level. It is easier to make certain that you have everything level if you perform the assembly with the legs upside down. (For help in making sure

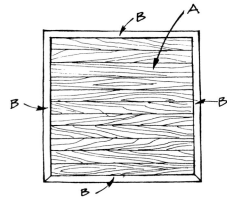

Figure 1

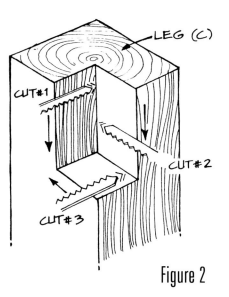

Figure 2

your project is perfectly level, see "Tips and Techniques.")

Carefully fit two of the side rails (D) inside the opening that you previously cut in the legs (C), matching the mitered ends. (Refer to *Figure 4*.) Glue and screw them in place using three 2-inch-long screws in each of the side rails (D). Repeat the process with the remaining three legs (C) and the remaining side rails (D).

5. Cut four triangular corner supports (E) from the 2 x 6 pine. These should measure 5-1/2 inches on the two short sides. Glue and screw them in each of the four corners, as shown in *Figure 4*, using four 3-inch-long screws in each corner support (E).

6. Cut four top trim pieces (F) from the 1 x 4 pine, each 50 inches long. Setting each piece on its face, miter both ends of each top trim piece (F) at a 45-degree angle as shown in *Figure 4*. Fasten the top trim pieces (F) to the legs (C) and to the side rails (D) using glue and screws. Use two 3-inch-long screws to connect each end of each top trim piece (F) to the legs (C). Use 2-inch-long screws spaced about 6 inches apart to connect the top trim piece (F) to the side rails (D). The top trim pieces (F) should overhang the legs by 1/2 inch on the edges.

Adding the Table Top

1. Set the assembled table top upside down on a level surface. Then place the assembled base upside down on top of it. Align the edges of the top trim pieces (F) with the table top assembly. Glue and screw them together. Screw through the top trim pieces (F) into the table top, as close as possible to the side rails (D). Use 1-1/4-inch-long screws spaced about 6 inches apart. Countersink the screws so that the screw heads can be covered by the molding to be added in the next step.

2. Cut four side trim pieces (G) from the decorative molding, each 42 inches long. Glue and screw them to the outside of the side rails (D) using one 1-1/4-inch-long screw every 6 inches. To avoid making holes in the molding, screw through the side rails (D) into the side trim pieces (G).

Finishing

1. Fill any cracks or crevices with filler, and thoroughly sand the assembled coffee table.

2. You can paint or stain the table the color of your choice. I applied a maple-toned stain to this table and let it dry thoroughly. Then I applied a light coat of white paint and, before it could dry, wiped most of the paint off. Finally, I finished it with several coats of varnish.

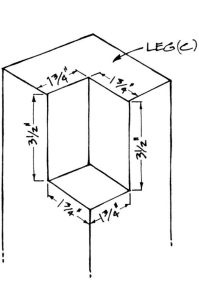

Figure 3

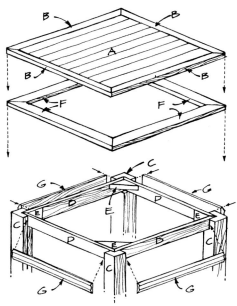

Figure 4

ENTRY HALL TABLE

The dimensions of this entry hall table (approximately 51 inches long by 12-1/2 inches wide by 26-1/2 inches high) make it extremely versatile. I use it alongside a staircase, but it would also be perfect behind a sofa or love seat.

28

MATERIALS LIST

Lumber:

1 pc. laminated 1 x 4 pine, 48" x 20"
(OR 25 linear ft. 1 x 4 pine)
33 linear ft. 1 x 4 pine
11 linear ft. 1 x 2 pine
11 linear ft. decorative molding—at least 3-1/2" wide x
    1" thick (top) and 3/4" thick (bottom)
9 linear ft. 2 x 2 pine
11 linear ft. very thin brass, 1-1/2" wide

Hardware:

approx. 100 #6 x 1-1/4" flathead wood screws
approx. 150 #6 x 2" flathead wood screws
approx. 75 3d finishing nails

Special Tools and Techniques:

2 or 3 heavy-duty bar clamps (optional)
bevels
miters

CUTTING LIST

Code	Description	Qty.	Material	Dimensions
A	Table Top	1	laminated pine	47-1/2" x 9"
B	Shelf	1	laminated pine	47-1/2" x 9"
C	Leg	8	1 x 4 pine	22-1/2" long
D	Short Leg Reinforcement	4	2 x 2 pine	8-1/2" long
E	Long Leg Reinforcement	4	2 x 2 pine	16" long
F	Short Shelf Trim	2	1 x 4 pine	3-1/2" long
G	Long Shelf Trim	2	1 x 4 pine	42" long
H	Short Table Trim	2	1 x 4 pine	9" long
I	Long Table Trim	2	1 x 4 pine	49" long
J	Long Molding	2	3-1/2" decorative molding	51" long
K	Short Molding	2	3-1/2" decorative molding	12-1/2" long
L	Long Brass Support	2	1 x 2 pine	51" long
M	Short Brass Support	2	1 x 2 pine	12-1/2" long

Making the Top and Shelf

The table top and the shelf are both constructed of laminated 1 x 4 pine boards. Most building-supply stores sell sections of pine that have already been laminated. If you want to laminate the boards yourself, you need 25 linear feet of 1 x 4 pine and at least two heavy-duty bar clamps.

1. If you purchased pine that is already laminated, simply cut two sections, each 47-1/2 by 9 inches, making the table top (A) and the shelf section (B). Then skip to "Constructing the Legs," below.

2. If you want to do the laminating yourself, cut three lengths of 1 x 4 pine, each 48 inches long, for the table top (A). To ensure a solid bond in the lamination process, it is a good idea to rip a minuscule amount from each edge to be laminated before gluing the wood lengths together. Then spread glue on the edges, and place the lengths of wood side by side. Clamp them together securely, using at least two bar clamps, and leave them overnight.

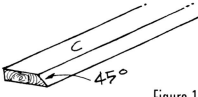

Figure 1

3. Trim the completed table top (A) to 47-1/2 by 9 inches.

4. Repeat the process described in steps 2 and 3 to construct the laminated shelf section (B), which is also 47-1/2 by 9 inches.

Constructing the Legs

1. Cut eight leg pieces (C) from 1 x 4 pine, each 22-1/2 inches long. Then set your saw blade to cut 45 degrees off vertical, and bevel one 22-1/2-inch-long edge of each of the legs (C) as shown in Figure 1.

2. Cut four short leg reinforcements (D) from 2 x 2 pine, each 8-1/2 inches long.

3. After wiping both beveled edges

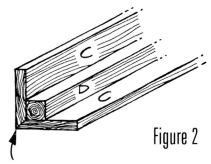

Figure 2

BEVEL JOINT

with glue, place two leg pieces (C) together, joining the bevels. Then attach one short leg reinforcement (D) to the inside of the beveled joint. Position the leg reinforcement (D) flush with the ends of the legs (C), as shown in Figure 2. Use glue and 2-inch-long screws for this assembly. Drive three screws into each of the two leg pieces (C).

4. Repeat Step 3 three more times to construct the remaining legs.

Adding the Shelf

1. Stand the four leg assemblies upright on a level surface with the short leg reinforcements (D) facing each other. Place the laminated shelf section (B) in the center of the leg assemblies so that it is resting on the leg reinforcements (D), as shown in Figure 3.

This operation is one that may require the assistance of a spouse or other willing helper because it is critical that all four leg assemblies remain level as you perform the next operation.

2. Apply glue on the surfaces to be joined, and screw through the laminated shelf (B) into the ends of the short leg reinforcements (D). Use two 2-inch screws at each corner of the laminated shelf (B).

3. Cut four long leg reinforcements (E) from 2 x 2 pine, each 16 inches long. Apply glue and use 2-inch-long screws to attach the long leg reinforcements (E) to the inside

edges of the beveled legs (C) above the laminated shelf (B). Use eight screws for each corner, putting four screws into each leg. As illustrated in *Figure 3*, the long leg reinforcements (E) extend 2-3/4 inches above the leg assemblies.

4. Cut two short shelf trim pieces (F) from 1 x 4 pine, each 3-1/2 inches long. Nail and glue them to the short sides of the laminated shelf (B), flush with the top of the shelf (B), as shown in *Figure 4*. Use about three 3-penny finishing nails on each short shelf trim piece (F).

5. Cut two long shelf trim pieces (G) from 1 x 4 pine, each 42 inches long. Nail and glue them to the long sides of the laminated shelf (B), flush with the top of the shelf (B). Space the nails about 6 inches apart.

Constructing the Table Top

1. First cut two short table trim pieces (H) from 1 x 4 pine, each 9 inches long. Then cut two long table trim pieces (I) from 1 x 4 pine, each 49 inches long.

2. Carefully set the laminated table top (A) upside down on a level surface. Now place one short table trim piece (H) on edge at each end of the table top (A), as shown in *Figure 5*. Use glue and three 1-1/4-inch-long screws to attach each short table trim piece (H) to the table top (A).

3. The long trim pieces (I) extend over the ends of the short trim pieces (H). *(See Figure 5.)* Attach the long trim (I) to the table top (A) with glue and screws. Use 1-1/4-inch-long screws spaced about 6 inches apart.

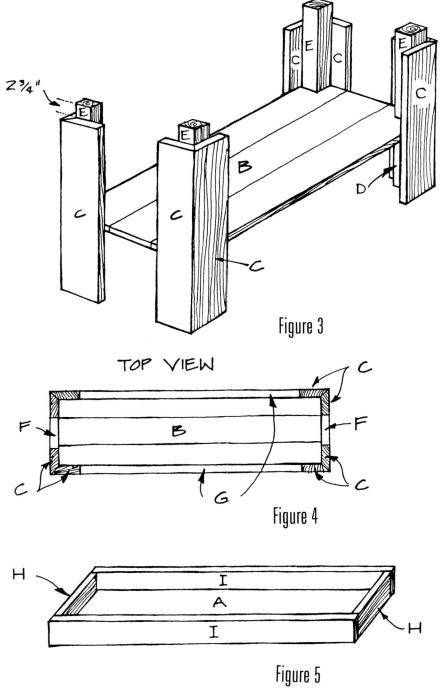

Figure 3

TOP VIEW

Figure 4

Figure 5

31

4. Set the completed table top onto the leg and shelf assembly. Make sure that the table trim pieces (H and I) rest on the legs (C) and that the table top (A) is supported by the long leg reinforcements (E).

5. Glue and screw through the long leg reinforcements (E) into both the long and short trim pieces (H and I) to secure the table top. Place two 2-inch-long screws in each of the corners.

Adding the Trim

The table structure is now complete. The remaining steps are to cover the table trim pieces (H and I) with decorative molding, attach support pieces for the brass, and attach the brass trim.

1. From the 3-1/2-inch-wide decorative molding, cut two long molding pieces (J), each 51 inches long, and two short molding pieces (K), each 12-1/2 inches long.

2. With each piece standing on edge, carefully miter the ends of each of the long and short molding pieces (J and K) at a 45-degree angle. Attach the molding pieces (J and K) to fit perfectly over the table trim pieces (H and I). Use glue and 3-penny finishing nails, placing one nail every 6 inches. Countersink the nails.

3. From 1 x 2 pine, cut two long brass support pieces (L), each 51 inches long, and two short brass support pieces (M), each 12-1/2 inches long.

4. Stand each of the brass support pieces (L and M) on edge and miter both ends at a 45-degree angle. Attach the mitered lengths just under the molding pieces (J and K). Use glue and finishing nails, spacing the nails about 6 inches apart. Countersink the nails.

Finishing the Table

1. Carefully fill any imperfections and nail holes with wood filler. Then sand the entire table.

2. Stain the table the color of your choice, and let the project dry overnight.

3. Attach the thin brass to the 1 x 2 brass support pieces (L and M) with glue suitable for both metal and wood; several brands are readily available. Since I planned to place the back of the table against a wall, I clamped the brass trim (positioned the joint) at the center back of the table and worked my way around. If you want to display the table where all four sides will be visible, you may want to begin at a corner and work your way around. To hide the joint where you begin and end the brass, purchase brass corner pieces to cover all four corners.

PLANT STAND

This plant stand is so practical and easy to build, you'll probably want several.
The finished size is 51 inches tall, but you could build several with varying heights to make a corner grouping. I used this one to display a prized wandering jew, but it would also be beautiful with a Boston fern or an asparagus fern.

PLANT STAND

MATERIALS LIST

Lumber:

17 linear ft. 1 x 6 pine
2 linear ft. 1 x 8 pine
2 linear ft. 1 x 10 pine

Hardware:

approx. 50 3d finishing nails
10-15 6d finishing nails

CUTTING LIST

Code	Description	Qty.	Material	Dimensions
A	Side	4	1 x 6 pine	48" long
B	Small Base	2	1 x 8 pine	7-1/4" long
C	Large Base	2	1 x 10 pine	9-1/4" long

Cutting the Pieces

1. Cut four side pieces (A) from 1 x 6 pine, each 48 inches long. It is very important to get a perfectly square cut on the ends; otherwise, you will have a "Leaning Tower of Plant" stand.

2. Cut two small base pieces (B) from 1 x 8 pine, each 7-1/4 inches long.

3. Cut two large base pieces (C) from 1 x 10 pine, each 9-1/4 inches long.

Assembly

1. Assemble the four side pieces (A), overlapping each piece in rotation as shown in *Figure 1*. With the four sides (A) in position, the stand measures 6-1/4 inches wide on all sides. Glue and nail all four sides (A) along their entire length. Use the smaller, 3-penny finishing nails, spacing them about 6 inches apart. Countersink the nails.

2. Center one small base (B) over one large base (C) as shown in *Figure 2*. Glue and nail the two pieces together using about four 3-penny finishing nails. Countersink the nails.

3. Repeat Step 2 using the remaining small base (B) and large base (C).

4. Center one base assembly on top of the stand. The large base should be facing up. *(See Figure 3.)* Use glue and the longer, 6-penny finishing nails to attach the base to the stand. Countersink the nails.

5. Turn the stand over and repeat Step 4 to attach the remaining base assembly to the stand.

Finishing

1. Fill any knotholes, cracks, or crevices with wood filler.

2. Sand the entire stand, and stain or paint the completed project the color of your choice.

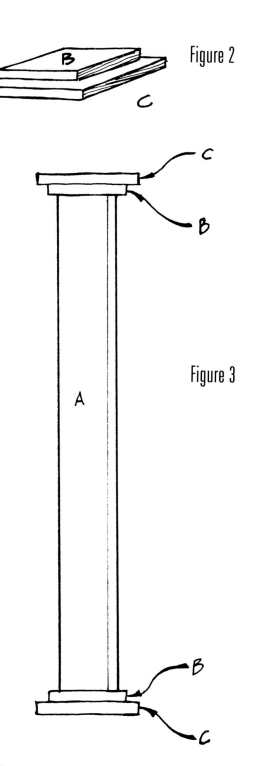

Figure 2

Figure 3

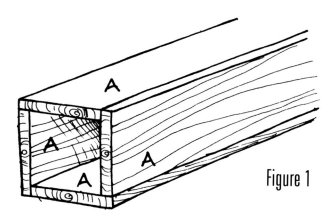

Figure 1

For years I sat on an extremely uncomfortable chair to apply my makeup. I finally replaced it with this sturdy seat, which is both attractive and comfortable. The finished size is 17 inches square and approximately 19 inches high, but the dimensions can be altered to suit your needs.

MATERIALS LIST

Lumber:

22 linear ft. 1 x 4 pine
5 linear ft. 3/4" x 3/4" pine strips
1 pc. 3/4" plywood, 16-1/2" sq.

Fabric and Notions:

1 pc. 2"-thick foam rubber, 17" sq.
(OR equivalent polyester batting)
3/4 yd. upholstery fabric
2 yds. decorative cotton cording, approx. 3/8" dia.

Hardware:

approx. 150 #6 x 1-1/4" flathead wood screws
upholstery tacks (optional)

Special Tools and Techniques:

staple gun (optional)
miters

UPHOLSTERED VANITY SEAT

CUTTING LIST

Code	Description	Qty.	Material	Dimensions
A	Leg	8	1 x 4 pine	16" long
B	Front/Back Connector	2	1 x 4 pine	14" long
C	Side Connector	2	1 x 4 pine	15-1/2" long
D	Front/Back Spacer	2	1 x 4 pine	8-1/2" long
E	Side Spacer	2	1 x 4 pine	10" long
F	Corner Support	4	1 x 4 pine	8-1/2" long
G	Leg Support	4	3/4" x 3/4" pine strips	12-1/2" long
H	Seat Bottom	1	3/4" plywood	16-1/2" sq.

Cutting the Parts

1. Cut all of the wooden parts listed in the "Cutting List," above, and label each one with its code letter.

Assembly

The seat frame consists of four sides. Although the finished project is square, it is clearer if we designate two sides, a front, and a back. The sides are identical to each other, and to the front and back. All of the components should be fastened together with both wood glue and screws, and each assembly should be checked carefully to make sure that the joints are perfectly square.

1. The construction of one side is shown in *Figure 1*. Attach two legs

Figure 1

(A) to one side connector (C), spacing them as shown. Note that the edges of the side connector are flush with the ends of the legs (A), and there is a 3/4-inch offset at each end of the side connector (C). Using glue and two 1-1/4-inch-long screws at each end of the side connector (C), attach both legs (A).

2. As shown in *Figure 1*, attach the side spacer (E) between the legs.

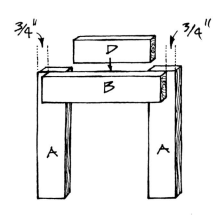

Figure 2

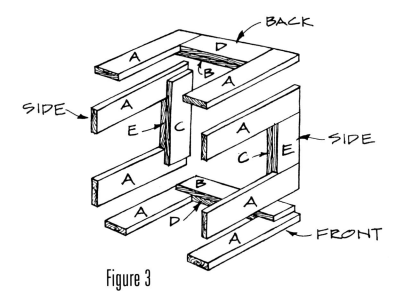

Figure 3

Apply glue, and use about three 1-1/4-inch-long screws, driving them through the side connector (C) into the side spacer (E).

3. Assemble the second side the same way you did the first, repeating Steps 1 and 2.

4. The front is shown in *Figure 2*. Assemble two legs (A) and one front/back connector (B), spacing them as shown. Again, the pieces are flush at the top, and there is a 3/4-inch offset at the sides. Use two screws at each end of the front/back connector (B) to secure the legs (A). Attach the front/back spacer (D) between the legs using three screws driven through the front/back connector (B) into the front/back spacer.

5. The back is a twin of the front; simply repeat Step 4.

6. The next step is to join the front, back, and sides. Attach the two sides to the front as shown in *Figure 3*, making certain that the legs are flush on both the top and bottom. Then attach the back to complete the frame. The side assemblies overlap the exposed ends of the front and back assemblies. Wipe glue on the adjoining edges, and, to make a solid connection, place a screw about every 6 inches at each joint.

7. Attach one leg support (G) to the inside corners of each of the four legs as shown in *Figure 4*. Use three or four screws on each side of each leg support (G).

8. Setting each corner support (F) on its face, miter both ends at a 45-degree angle as shown in *Figure 5*.

9. Referring to *Figure 6*, attach the mitered corner supports (F), making sure that they are flush with the top edges of the assembled frame. Screw through the edges of the corner supports (F) at an angle (toenail) into the front, back, and side connectors (B and C).

10. Patch any crevices or gaps in the completed frame with wood putty (or spackle) and sand it. Paint (or stain) it the color of your choice, and seal it with an appropriate finish coat.

Making the Seat Cushion

1. The 16-1/2-inch-square piece of plywood is used for the seat bottom (H). Position the 17-inch-square piece of foam rubber (or equivalent polyester batting) in the center of the seat bottom (H), and glue it in place.

2. Center the upholstery fabric over the foam rubber, wrap the fabric over the edge of the seat bottom (H), and staple (or tack) it to the underside. You can minimize the number of wrinkles if you first staple the center of one side, then the center of the opposite side, and, finally, work your way out to the corners. Smooth the fabric as you go. Staple the centers of the remaining sides, and again work your way to the corners. Be generous with the staples; use enough to keep the fabric from puckering along the sides.

3. To attach the upholstered seat cushion to the frame, place the seat cushion upside down on a flat surface with the frame upside down on top of it. Screw through the center of each of the corner supports (F) into the seat bottom (H) using 1-1/4-inch-long screws spaced about 6 inches apart.

4. Glue the cording between the seat cushion and the frame, beginning in the center of one side and working around the entire seat.

5. Now pat yourself on the back for a job well done!

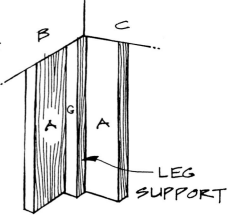

Figure 4

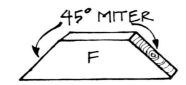

Figure 5

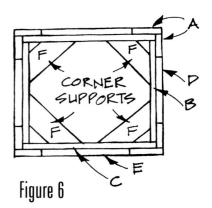

Figure 6

This upholstered bench can be used in a variety of places in your house. At the foot of your bed, it holds quilts and provides comfortable seating. You can also place it against the wall to create a cozy retreat in any room. The finished size is 48 inches long, 13 inches wide, and approximately 18 inches high.

MATERIALS LIST

Lumber:

9 linear ft. 2 x 2 pine
10 linear ft. 2 x 4 pine
1 pc. 3/4" plywood, 4' sq.

Fabric and Notions:

4 yds. upholstery fabric, 60" wide
1 pc. 1-1/2-inch-thick foam rubber, 13" x 48"
(OR equivalent polyester quilt batting)

Hardware:

approx. 75 #6 x 1-1/4" flathead wood screws
approx 100 #6 x 2" flathead wood screws
approx. 50 #10 x 3" flathead wood screws
upholstery tacks (optional)

Special Tools and Techniques:

staple gun (optional)

CUTTING LIST

Code	Description	Qty.	Material	Dimensions
A	Vertical Leg	4	2 x 2 pine	13" long
B	Horizontal Leg	4	2 x 2 pine	13" long
C	Side	2	3/4" plywood	13" x 16-3/4"
D	Bottom	1	3/4" plywood	13" x 46-1/2"
E	Bottom Support	2	2 x 4 pine	43-1/2" long
F	Center Support	1	2 x 4 pine	6" long
G	Corner Support	4	2 x 4 pine	3-1/2" x 3-1/2" x 5"
H	Leg Panel	4	upholstery fabric	20" x 42"
I	Bottom Panel	2	upholstery fabric	4-1/4" x 15"
J	Front/Back Panel	4	upholstery fabric	9" x 57"
K	Bench Top	1	3/4" plywood	12-1/2" x 47-1/2"
L	Top Panel	1	upholstery fabric	17" x 54"

Making the Legs

1. From 2 x 2 pine, cut four vertical leg pieces (A), each 13 inches long, and four horizontal leg pieces (B), each 13 inches long.

2. Cut two side pieces (C) from 3/4-inch-thick plywood, each measuring 13 by 16-3/4 inches.

3. To assemble one leg, first attach two vertical leg pieces (A) to two horizontal leg pieces (B) as shown in *Figure 1*. Then attach the leg assembly to one side piece (C). Glue and screw them together using 2-inch-long screws spaced about 6 inches apart. Note that the side piece (C) extends 3/4 inch beyond the edge of one horizontal leg piece (B).

4. Repeat Step 3 to assemble the second leg.

Figure 1

UPHOLSTERED BENCH

Assembling the Bench

1. Cut one 13-inch by 46-1/2-inch bottom bench piece (D) from 3/4-inch-thick plywood.

2. Cut two bottom support pieces (E) from 2 x 4 pine, each 43-1/2 inches long.

3. Place the bottom bench piece (D) upside down on a level surface. Fit the assembled legs onto the bottom bench piece (D) as shown in *Figure 2*. The bottom bench piece (D) should fit within the plywood extensions on the side pieces (C) of the leg assemblies, as illustrated. Glue and screw both the plywood extensions and the horizontal leg pieces (B) to the bottom bench piece (D) using 2-inch-long screws spaced about 6 inches apart. Screw through the bottom bench piece (D) into the horizontal leg pieces (B).

4. Fit the bottom supports (E) between the legs, and glue and screw them to the bottom bench piece (D), as shown in *Figure 2*. Use 1-1/4-inch-long screws placed every 6 inches. Screw through the bottom bench piece (D) into the bottom supports (E).

5. Cut one 6-inch-long center support (F) from 2 x 4 pine.

6. Fit the center support (F) between the bottom support pieces (E), and secure it in place with glue and screws. Screw through the bottom bench piece (D) into the center support (F) using 1-1/4-inch-long screws placed every 3 inches. Use two 3-inch screws driven at an angle (toenail) through both ends of the center support (F) into the bottom support (E).

7. Cut four triangular corner supports (G) from 2 x 4 pine, each measuring 3-1/2 by 3-1/2 by 5 inches. Glue and screw them to the horizontal leg pieces (B) and the bottom supports (E). Use about four 3-inch-long screws on each corner support (G)—two screws into the bottom support (E) and two screws into the horizontal leg piece (B). See *Figure 2*.

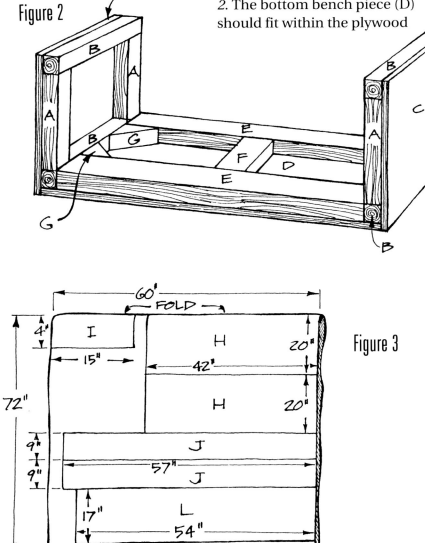

Figure 2

Figure 3

Covering the Legs

1. The first step is to sew a gathered "sock" for each of the legs. A fabric-cutting diagram is shown in *Figure 3*. All seams are sewn 1 inch wide. Cut four leg panels (H) from the upholstery fabric, each measuring 20 by 42 inches.

2. Cut two bottom panels (I) from the upholstery fabric, each measuring 4-1/4 by 15 inches.

3. Placing right sides together, sew a 1-inch-wide seam along both 20-inch-long edges of two leg panels (H) to form a tube *(Figure 4)*.

4. Sew a long gathering stitch along both long edges of the tube *(Figure 4)*. Gather one side of the tube evenly, and pin it to one bottom panel (I), adjusting the gathers to fit, and placing right sides together. Position a tube seam at the center of each long edge of the bottom panel (I), and adjust the gathers to conceal the seams. Sew a seam completely around the bottom panel (I), as shown in *Figure 5*.

5. Turn the completed "sock" right side out. Pull the gathers on the open edge, and fit the sock over one assembled bench leg as shown in *Figure 6*.

6. Make certain that the bottom panel (I) is positioned evenly over the bottom of the leg. Pull the gathered top of the sock up and attach the fabric to the bottom bench piece (D). You can secure the fabric to the wood with a staple gun, or you can use upholstery tacks and a tack hammer. Begin on the outside of the leg at the middle, and work toward the edges. Don't be stingy with the staples; make certain that the gathers are held securely in place.

7. Turn the bench upside down, and attach the inner section of the gathered sock to the bottom bench (D), carefully working it over the 2 x 4 supports. Clip and fold the fabric as necessary to make the gathers neat and evenly spaced around the leg. The most critical part of this procedure is to make certain that the fabric completely covers the junction of the horizontal leg pieces (B) and the bottom supports (E).

8. Repeat steps 3 through 7 to cover the remaining leg.

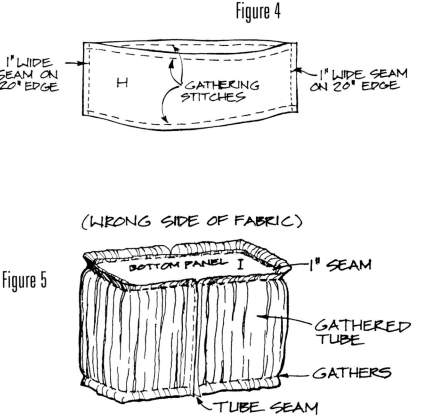

Figure 4

1" WIDE SEAM ON 20" EDGE

H

GATHERING STITCHES

1" WIDE SEAM ON 20" EDGE

(WRONG SIDE OF FABRIC)

Figure 5

BOTTOM PANEL I

1" SEAM

GATHERED TUBE

GATHERS

TUBE SEAM

43

Covering the Front and Back

1. Cut four front/back panels (J) from the upholstery fabric, each measuring 9 by 57 inches.

2. Place two front/back panels (J) right sides together, and sew a seam along one 9-inch end to form a single panel measuring 9 x 112 inches.

3. Sew long gathering stitches along both 112-inch edges of the combined panel.

4. Pull the gathers evenly along both long edges until the fabric panel measures 48 inches long. Fold under the raw ends on the short edges (it helps to iron them), and attach the fabric panel to the underside of the bench, flush with the plywood. Use staples or upholstery tacks to secure the fabric in place. Again, don't be stingy with the staples since they must hold the gathers in place.

5. Pull the fabric panel over the front of the bench and attach it to the top, again using staples or tacks.

6. Repeat steps 2 through 5 to cover the remaining support piece (E) on the back of the bench.

Figure 6

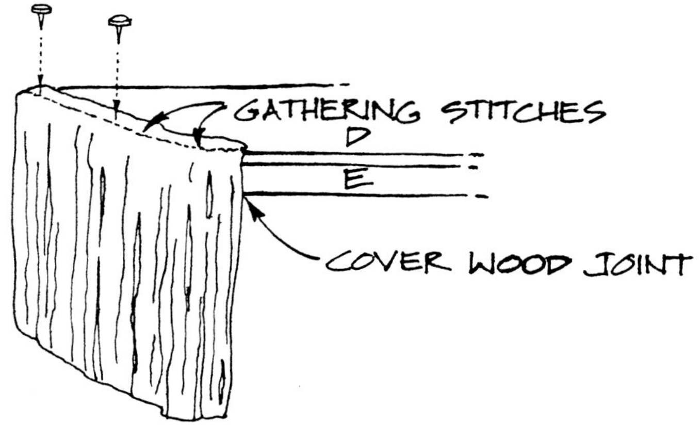

GATHERING STITCHES
D
E
COVER WOOD JOINT

Finishing

1. Cut one 12-1/2-inch by 47-1/2-inch bench top (K) from 3/4-inch-thick plywood.

2. If your piece of 1-1/2-inch-thick foam rubber is larger than 13 by 48 inches, trim it to those dimensions.

3. Center the foam rubber (or an equivalent amount of polyester quilt batting) over the plywood bench top (J) and glue it in place.

4. Cut one 17-inch by 54-inch top panel (L) from the upholstery fabric.

5. Centering the top panel (L) over the foam rubber, staple or tack it to the underside of the plywood bench top (K). (You can minimize the number of wrinkles if you start by stapling the center of one long side and the center of the opposite long side. Then work your way out to the ends, smoothing the fabric as you go. Use enough staples to hold the fabric securely. Next, staple the center of both ends, and again work your way out to the corners.)

6. Attach the upholstered bench cushion to the frame. Place the bench cushion upside down on a flat surface, and put the assembled bench upside down on top of it. Screw through the plywood in the bench into the plywood bench top (K) using 1-1/4-inch-long screws. Place one screw in each corner and as many additional screws along the length as necessary to pull the plywood bench top (K) evenly onto the bottom (D).

BASIC BOOKCASE

No matter how many bookcases you have, it seems as though you always need just one more. I put this one in a hallway to hold books and knickknacks. In fact, I'm thinking about building another one for the guest bedroom, and it would be nice to have another in my closet, and one in the utility room, and another....

BASIC BOOKCASE

MATERIALS LIST

Lumber:

15 linear ft. 1 x 10 pine
2 linear ft. box molding, 1-3/4" wide
1 pc. 1/4" plywood, approx. 26" x 42" (optional)

Hardware:

approx. 50 #6 x 1-1/4" flathead wood screws
additional 50 screws to add plywood back (optional)
approx. 20 6d finishing nails

Special Tools and Techniques:

framing square
2 or 3 bar clamps (optional)

CUTTING LIST

Code	Description	Qty.	Material	Dimensions
A	Side	2	1 x 10 pine	41" long
B	Shelf	4	1 x 10 pine	24" long
C	Trim	1	box molding	24" long
D	Back Panel (optional)	1	1/4" plywood	25-1/2" x 41"

Cutting the Pieces

Cut two sides (A), four shelves (B), and one trim piece (C) according to the specifications given in the "Cutting List," above.

Assembly

This is a very simple project, and the only critical part of the assembly is to mark the shelf placements accurately. Take time to do this correctly and use a framing square; otherwise, your shelves will slant (and it will be difficult to store marbles on them).

1. *Figure 1* shows the marking layout for placing the shelves. Set the two sides (A) next to each other, and simultaneously mark the position for all of the shelves completely across both sides.

2. Glue and screw the four shelves (B) between the two sides (A) as shown in *Figure 2*, carefully aligning each shelf with the marks you made in Step 1. I used three screws on each end of each shelf, but you can add more if the shelves feel unsteady. Just be sure to space them evenly apart. It helps to use bar clamps to hold the assembly

together (this prevents any shifting) while you are inserting the screws.

3. As an optional step, if you want to store lots of books or other heavy objects, you can add a piece of 1/4-inch-thick plywood to the back of the bookcase for additional reinforcement. Construct a back panel (D) by trimming the plywood to match the full dimensions of the finished bookcase—41 inches high by 25-1/2 inches wide. Attach the back panel (D) to the rear side of the bookcase by screwing it into the edges of the sides (A) and shelves (B). Use 1-1/4-inch-long screws spaced about 6 inches apart.

4. Glue and nail the trim piece (C) under the bottom shelf (B), flush with the front edge, as shown in *Figure 2*. Use 6-penny finishing nails spaced about every six inches, nailing through the lower shelf (B). Also nail through the sides (A) into the trim piece (C). Countersink all of the nails.

5. Use wood filler to fill any cracks and crevices. Sand the completed bookcase.

6. Paint or stain the bookcase the color of your choice.

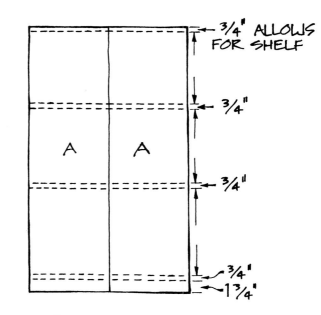

Figure 1

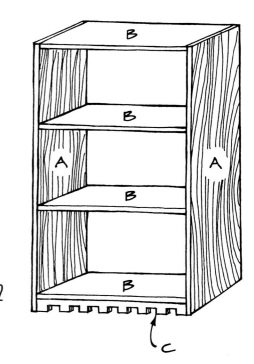

Figure 2

47

With its simple beauty and clean lines, this easy-to-build chest resembles Shaker furniture. It is perfect for storing extra blankets, pillows, and sheets. Made with a laminated pine top, it's quick to construct, and sturdy enough to use as a seat. The finished size is about 20 inches tall, 19-1/2 inches deep, and 51-1/2 inches wide.

MATERIALS LIST

Lumber:

1 sheet 3/4" plywood (4' x 8')*
17 linear ft. 2 x 2 pine
46 linear ft. 1 x 4 pine
1 pc. laminated 1 x 4 pine, 19-1/2" x 51-1/2"
(OR 26 linear ft. 1 x 4 pine)

Hardware:

approx. 200 #6 x 1-1/4" flathead wood screws
approx. 125 #6 x 2" flathead wood screws
4' brass piano hinge
4 brass corner pieces

Special Tools and Techniques:

2 or 3 bar clamps (optional)
bevels
miters

*See "Notes on the Materials," below.

CUTTING LIST

Code	Description	Qty.	Material	Dimensions
A	Side	2	3/4" plywood	16-1/2" x 15-1/2"
B	Corner Support	4	2 x 2 pine	14-1/4" long
C	Front/Back	2	3/4" plywood	16-1/2" x 48"
D	Bottom	1	3/4" plywood	46-1/2" x 15-1/2"
E	Long Reinforcement	2	2 x 2 pine	46-1/2" long
F	Short Reinforcement	2	2 x 2 pine	12-1/2" long
G	Vertical Trim	8	1 x 4 pine	19" long
H	Leg Supports	4	2 x 2 pine	2-1/2" long
I	Long Horizontal Trim	4	1 x 4 pine	42-1/2" long
J	Short Horizontal Trim	4	1 x 4 pine	11-1/2" long
K	Long Top Trim	2	1 x 4 pine	49-1/2" long
L	Short Top Trim	2	1 x 4 pine	18-1/2" long
M	Top	1	laminated pine	19-1/2" x 51-1/2"
N	Top Brace	2	1 x 4 pine	16" long

Notes on the Materials

Because I wanted a natural finish on this chest, I used stain-grade plywood. If you plan to paint yours, you can use lower grade, less expensive material.

The top of this chest is constructed of laminated 1 x 4 pine boards. Most building-supply stores sell sections of pine that have already been laminated. If you want to laminate the boards yourself, you need 26 linear feet of 1 x 4 pine and at least two bar clamps.

Constructing the Basic Box

1. Cut two side pieces (A) from 3/4-inch-thick plywood, each measuring 16-1/2 by 15-1/2 inches.

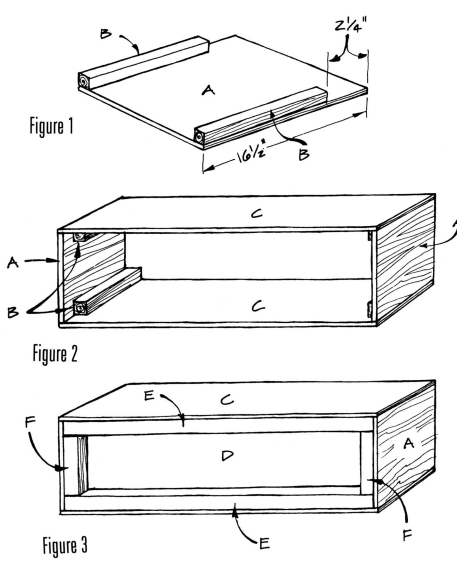

Figure 1

Figure 2

Figure 3

2. Cut four corner supports (B) from 2 x 2 pine, each 14-1/4 inches long.

3. Refer to *Figure 1*, and attach one corner support (B) flush with each 16-1/2-inch edge of one side (A). Note that the corner support (B) is positioned flush at one end and is 2-1/4 inches short at the other end, as shown in *Figure 1*. This 2-1/4 inch gap will accommodate the addition of the bottom of the chest and the supports underneath. Use glue and 2-inch-long screws placed about every 4 inches. Screw through the side (A) into the corner support (B). Although you don't need to countersink these screws because they will be covered by trim, be sure to drive them all the way into the wood so that the screw heads don't protrude.

4. Repeat step 3 to attach the remaining two corner supports (B) to the other side (A).

5. Cut two front/back pieces (C) from 3/4-inch-thick plywood, each measuring 16-1/2 by 48 inches.

6. Place the two sides (A) opposite each other, with the 2-1/4-inch gap at the bottom of both sides (A). Glue and screw the sides (A) to both the front and back (C), matching 16-1/2-inch edges, as shown in *Figure 2*. The front and back pieces (C) should overlap the exposed edges of the sides (A). Use 2-inch-long screws placed about every 4 inches, and screw through the front and back (C) into the corner supports (B).

Adding the Bottom

1. Cut one 46-1/2-inch by 15-1/2-inch bottom (D) from 3/4-inch-thick plywood.

2. Turn the assembly upside down so that the 2-1/4-inch offsets are at the top. Then fit the bottom (D) inside the front, back, and sides (A and C), resting it on the ends of the four corner supports (B). Glue and screw the bottom in place at all four corners using one 2-inch-long screw in each corner. This will hold the bottom in place until you add the reinforcements.

3. Cut two long reinforcements (E) from 2 x 2 pine, each 46-1/2 inches long.

4. Cut two short reinforcements (F) from 2 x 2 pine, each 12-1/2 inches long.

5. Glue and screw one long re-inforcement (E) in place, flush against the bottom (D) and front or back (C), as shown in *Figure 3*. Screw through the front or back (C) into the long reinforcement (E). Use 2-inch-long screws and space them about 4 inches apart.

6. Repeat step 5 to attach the remaining long reinforcement (E).

7. Turn the assembly right side up. Now screw through the bottom (D) into each of the long reinforcements (E), placing one 2-inch-long screw about every 5 inches.

8. Following the same procedures as you used in steps 5 through 7,

glue and screw the two short reinforcements (F) between the long reinforcements (E). Again refer to *Figure 3*.

Adding the Trim

1. The vertical trim serves two purposes: it covers the exposed edges of the front and back (C,) and it extends down from the basic box to form legs.

2. Cut eight vertical trim pieces (G) from 1 x 4 pine, each 19 inches long.

3. Set your saw blade to cut at 45 degrees off vertical, and bevel one 19-inch-long edge of each of the eight vertical trim pieces (G) as shown in *Figure 4*.

4. Attach two of the vertical trim pieces (G) to each corner of the assembly, matching the beveled edges as shown in *Figure 5*. Note that the vertical trim pieces (G) are flush at the top with the front, back, and sides (C and A), and extend 2-1/2 inches past the bottom. Wipe glue on all of the surfaces to be joined, and use 1-1/4-inch screws placed about every 4 inches. To avoid having screw holes on the

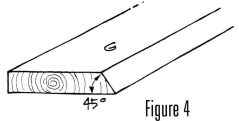

Figure 4

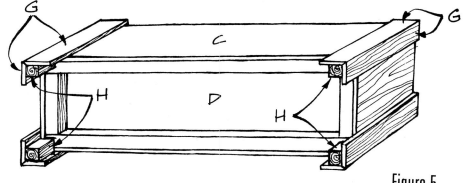

Figure 5

51

outside, screw from the inside of the chest through the front, back, and sides into the vertical trim (G).

5. Cut four leg supports (H) from 2 x 2 pine, each 2-1/2 inches long.

6. Glue and screw one leg support (H) to the inside of each leg formed by the vertical trim (G), as shown in *Figure 5*. Screw through the leg support (H) into the vertical trim (G) using two 2-inch-long screws on each side of each leg support (H).

7. Cut four long horizontal trim pieces (I) from 1 x 4 pine, each 42-1/2 inches long.

8. Glue and screw one long horizontal trim piece (I) between the two vertical trim pieces (G), putting it flush with the top of the front (C), as shown in *Figure 6*. Again, to avoid screw holes on the outside, screw through the inside of the front (C) into the long horizontal trim piece (I). Use 1-1/4-inch-long screws placed about every 5 inches.

9. Glue and screw a second long horizontal trim piece (I) flush with the bottom of the front (C), as shown in *Figure 6*. Again, screw

through the inside of the front (C) into the long horizontal trim pieces (I), and use 1-1/4-inch-long screws spaced about 5 inches apart.

10. Repeat steps 8 and 9 to attach the remaining two long horizontal trim pieces (I) to the back (C).

11. Cut four short horizontal trim pieces (J) from 1 x 4 pine, each 11-1/2 inches long.

12. Glue and screw one short horizontal trim piece (J) between the two vertical trim pieces (G), placing it flush with the top of one side (A) as shown in *Figure 6*. Once again, screw through the side (A) into the short horizontal trim piece (J). Use 1-1/4-inch-long screws placed about 5 inches apart.

13. Glue and screw a second short horizontal trim piece (J) flush with the bottom of the side (A), as shown in *Figure 6*. Screw through the inside of the side (A) into the short horizontal trim piece (J), and use 1-1/4-inch-long screws placed about 5 inches apart.

14. Repeat steps 12 and 13 to attach the remaining two short horizontal trim pieces (J) to the remaining side (A).

Adding the Top Trim

The top trim is a 1 x 4 pine frame that covers the exposed edges at the top of the chest.

1. From 1 x 4 pine, cut two long top trim pieces (K), each 49-1/2 inches long, and two short top trim pieces (L), each 18-1/2 inches long.

Figure 6

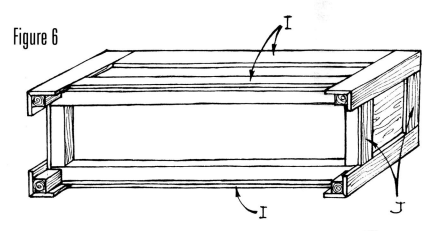

2. Setting each top trim piece (K and L) on its face, miter both ends at a 45-degree angle.

3. Fit the mitered trim pieces (K and L) onto the top of the chest, carefully matching the miters. Glue and screw them in place using 1-1/4-inch-long screws. Screw through the top trim pieces (K and L) into the long and short horizontal trim pieces (I and J). Countersink the screws.

Installing the Top

1. If you purchased material already laminated, trim the piece to 19-1/2 by 51-1/2 inches to make the top (M). Then skip down to step 4.

2. To make the laminated top (M) yourself, cut six lengths of 1 x 4 pine, each 51-1/2 inches long. Before gluing the wood lengths together, rip a minuscule amount from each edge to ensure a solid bond in the lamination process. Then spread glue on the adjoining edges, and place the lengths of wood side by side. Clamp them together securely, using at least two bar clamps, and leave them clamped overnight.

3. Trim the laminated section to make one top (M) measuring 19-1/2 by 51-1/2 inches.

4. Sand every surface of the laminated top (M) thoroughly. Examine both faces of the top (M), and choose the better-looking one for the outside.

5. Cut two top braces (N) from 1 x 4 pine, each 16 inches long.

6. Attach the two top braces (N) to the inside face of the top (M). As shown in *Figure 7*, center the top braces between the long edges of the top, and place each one 15 inches in from the short sides of the top. Use glue and 1-1/4-inch-long screws spaced about 4 inches apart to secure the braces to the top.

Finishing

1. Fill all exposed screw holes with wood filler.

2. Sand the chest assembly thoroughly.

3. Install the top (M) onto the chest using a 4-foot-long piano hinge. The hinge is screwed into the long top trim (K) and the inside back edge of the top (M). The hinge should be installed so that the back edge of the top (M) is flush with the back of the chest. The top overhangs the front and sides of the chest by 1 inch.

4. Stain or paint the completed project the color of your choice. I used a maple-colored stain.

5. Attach the brass corner trim to all four corners of the finished chest.

Figure 7

SWEATER CABINET

Almost anyone can use an extra cabinet in the bedroom, the closet, or any other room. I needed more space to store my sweaters, and this pretty addition to my bedroom has two shelves inside, providing lots of room. Made with laminated pine sides, back, and top, the cabinet doesn't take long to build, and the elegant-looking paneled door is easier to construct than you might expect. The finished cabinet is approximately 22 inches wide, 12 inches deep, and 44 inches tall.

MATERIALS LIST

Lumber:

4 pcs. laminated pine:
   2 pcs. 10-1/2" x 35-1/2"
   1 pc. 18-1/4" x 35-1/2"
   1 pc. 11" x 20-3/4"
(OR 43 linear ft. 1 x 4 pine)
13 linear ft. 1 x 4 pine
5 linear ft. 1 x 10 pine
3 linear ft. 1 x 2 pine
12 linear ft. 2 x 4 pine
5 linear ft. 1 x 8 pine

Hardware:

approx. 75 #6 x 1-1/4" flathead wood screws
approx. 20 #6 x 2" flathead wood screws
approx. 50 #6 x 2-1/2" flathead wood screws
approx. 25 8d finishing nails
2 concealed hinges*
1 door pull
1 magnetic cabinet catch (optional)

Special Tools and Techniques:

2 or 3 bar clamps (optional)
miters
bevels
dadoes

*See "Notes on the Materials," below.

CUTTING LIST

Code	Description	Qty.	Material	Dimensions
A	Side	2	laminated pine	10-1/2" x 35-1/2"
B	Back	1	laminated pine	18-1/4" x 35-1/2"
C	Top	1	laminated pine	11 x 20-3/4"
D	Bottom	1	1 x 10 pine, ripped	18-1/4" long
E	Shelf	2	1 x 10 pine, ripped	18-1/4" long
F	Shelf Support	4	1 x 2 pine	8-7/8" long
G	Lower Base Side	2	2 x 4 pine, ripped	10-1/2" long
H	Lower Base Front/Back	2	2 x 4 pine, ripped	19-3/4" long
I	Upper Base Front/Back	2	2 x 4 pine	21-3/4" long
J	Upper Base Side	2	2 x 4 pine	11-1/2" long
K	Panel	4	1 x 8 pine	7" x 14-5/8"
L	Side Frame	2	1 x 4 pine, ripped	35-1/2" long
M	Top/Bottom Frame	2	1 x 4 pine, ripped	18" long
N	Inner Frame	3	1 x 4 pine, ripped	14" long

Notes on the Materials

The two sides, back, and top of this cabinet are constructed from laminated 1 x 4 pine. Most building-supply stores sell sections of pine that have already been laminated. If you want to laminate the sections yourself, you need a total of 43 linear feet of 1 x 4 pine and two or three bar clamps.

I used concealed hinges for this cabinet because I wanted the hinges to be invisible from the outside. If you don't mind seeing the pin portion of the hinge when the cabinet is closed, you can substitute butt hinges. I don't recommend using surface-mounted hinges for this project.

Making the Cabinet Sides, Back, and Top

1. If you purchased material that is already laminated, simply cut two sides (A) each 10-1/2 by 35-1/2 inches, one back (B) 18-1/4 by 35-1/2 inches, and one top (C) 11 by 20-3/4 inches. Then skip down to "Making the Bottom and the Shelves," below.

If you laminate the boards yourself, it is a good idea to rip a minuscule amount from each edge to be joined before gluing the wood lengths together. Use this procedure in each of the following assemblies to ensure a solid bond in the lamination process.

2. To assemble the laminated sides (A), cut six boards from 1 x 4 pine, each 35-1/2 inches long.

3. After ripping each edge to be joined, place three of the boards side by side. Wipe glue on the adjoining 35-1/2-inch-long edges, and clamp the three boards together using at least two bar clamps. (Refer to the "Tips and Techniques" section if you need assistance with clamping procedures.) Leave the assembly clamped for at least 24 hours. You now have one side (A) measuring 10-1/2 by 35-1/2 inches.

4. Repeat step 3 to assemble the second side (A).

5. To make one laminated back (B), cut six boards from 1 x 4 pine, each 35-1/2 inches long.

6. After ripping the edges to be joined, place the six boards side by side. Wipe glue on the adjoining 35-1/2-inch-long edges, and clamp the six boards together with two or three bar clamps. Leave the assembly clamped for at least 24 hours.

7. You now have a laminated section that measures 21 by 35-1/2 inches. Rip one long side of the lamination to make a back (B) measuring 18-1/4 by 35-1/2 inches.

8. To assemble the laminated top (C), cut four boards from 1 x 4 pine, each 20-3/4 inches long.

9. After ripping the edges to be joined, place the four boards side by side. Wipe glue on the adjoining

Figure 1

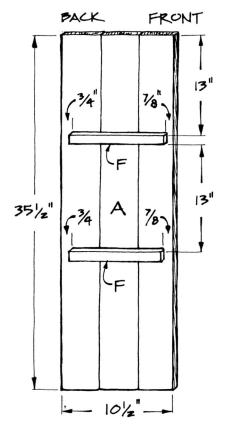

56

20-3/4-inch-long edges, and clamp the four boards together with bar clamps. Leave the assembly clamped for at least 24 hours.

10. You how have a laminated section that measures 14 by 20-3/4 inches. Rip one short side of the lamination to make one top (C) measuring 11 by 20-3/4 inches.

Making the Bottom and the Shelves

The cabinet bottom (D) and two shelves (E) are identical. Each measures 8-7/8 by 18-1/4 inches.

1. Rip a total of five feet of 1 x 10 pine to a width of 8-7/8 inches.

2. Cut one cabinet bottom (D) and two shelves (E) from the ripped 1 x 10 pine, each 18-1/4 inches long.

3. The two shelves (E) are supported by shelf supports (F) that are screwed to the inside of the cabinet sides. The spacing of the shelves inside the cabinet is at your discretion. I placed the first shelf 13 inches from the top, and the second one 13 inches below that. *Figure 1* shows the placement of the shelf supports.

4. Cut four shelf supports (F) from 1 x 2 pine, each 8-7/8 inches long.

5. According to the spacing that you desire, mark the placement of the shelf supports (F) on the inside face of each of the sides (A). Referring to

Figure 1, note that the shelf supports (F) are installed 3/4 inch from the rear edge of the sides (A) in order to accommodate the back (B). There is a 7/8-inch space at the front ends of the shelf supports (F) to allow for the door.

6. Glue and screw the two shelf supports (F) to the inside face of each side (A) using two 1-1/4-inch-long screws on each shelf support. The two sides with the shelf supports attached should be mirror images of each other.

Assembling the Cabinet

1. *Figure 2* shows the assembly of the cabinet. Note that the cabinet top, back, and sides are all flush at the rear, and that the top overhangs the sides and front by 1/2 inch. The bottom fits inside the cabinet like a bottom shelf. Use glue and screws on all of the assembly steps, and countersink the screws.

2. Place the back (B) between the two sides (A). Screw through the sides (A) into the edges of the back (B) using 1-1/4-inch-long screws spaced about 5 inches apart.

3. Fit the bottom (D) between the two sides (A) so that it is flush with the lower edges of the sides. Screw through the sides (A) into the edges of the bottom (D) using three 1-1/4-inch-long screws on each side. Also use three 1-1/4-inch-long screws through the back (B) into the edge of the bottom (D).

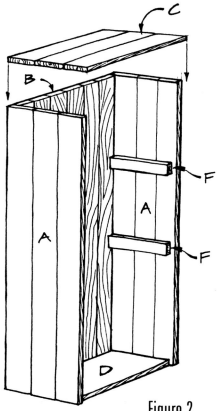

Figure 2

4. Fit the top (C) onto the cabinet. It should be flush with the cabinet assembly at the back and overhang the front and sides by 1/2 inch. Screw through the top (C) into the edges of the sides (A) and into the edge of the back (B). Use 1-1/4-inch-long screws placed about every 5 inches.

Building the Base

As shown in *Figure 3*, the base of the cabinet is an assembly of two mitered frames built from 2 x 4s. Note that the smaller frame on the bottom is made with the 2 x 4s standing on edge, and that the larger, upper frame is assembled with the 3-1/2-inch width placed horizontally. The top of the base extends 1 inch beyond the cabinet on the front and sides, and is flush with the cabinet in the back.

1. Rip a total of 5-1/2 feet of 2 x 4 pine to a width of 2 inches.

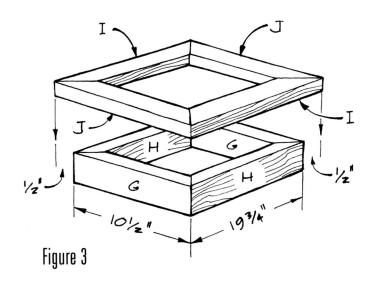

Figure 3

2. Cut two lower base side pieces (G) from the ripped 2 x 4, each 10-1/2 inches long.

3. With each lower base side piece (G) standing on edge, miter both ends at a 45-degree angle.

4. Cut two lower base front/back pieces (H) from the ripped 2 x 4, each 22-1/2 inches long.

5. Again, stand the pieces on edge, and miter both ends of each of the lower base front/back pieces (H) at a 45-degree angle.

6. Assemble the two lower base front/back pieces (H) and the two lower base side pieces (G), matching the mitered corners, as shown in *Figure 3*. Glue and screw the corners together using two 2-1/2-inch-long screws in each corner.

7. Cut two upper base front/back pieces (I) from full-width 2 x 4 pine, each 21-3/4 inches long.

8. Setting each upper base front/back piece (I) on its face, miter both ends at a 45-degree angle as shown in *Figure 3*.

9. Cut two upper base side pieces (J) from 2 x 4 pine, each 11-1/2 inches long.

10. Again, with each piece on its face, miter both ends of each upper base side piece (J) at a 45-degree angle as shown in *Figure 3*.

11. Assemble the two upper base front/back pieces (I) and the two

upper base side pieces (J), matching the mitered corners, as shown in *Figure 3*. Glue and screw the corners together using one 2-1/2-inch-long screw in each corner.

12. An optional step at this point is to rout a decorative design on the outer edges of the assembled upper base. I routed the top outer edge, turned the base upside down, and routed the bottom outer edge with a matching cut.

13. Place the assembled upper base on top of the lower base. The two base assemblies are flush at the back, and the upper base overhangs the lower base by 1 inch on the sides and front. Glue and screw the two base frames together. Screw through the upper base into the lower base using 2-1/2-inch-long screws placed about every 4 inches. Countersink the screws.

Attaching the Cabinet to the Base

1. Turn the cabinet assembly upside down. Set the base assembly onto the bottom of the cabinet so that the upper base fits next to the cabinet assembly. The upper base is flush with the cabinet at the back and overhangs the sides and front by 1 inch.

2. Screw through the upper base boards (I and J) into the bottom of the cabinet using several 2-inch-long screws.

Constructing the Door

Although it looks very professional, the raised-panel door is not difficult to make. Just take your time and measure the pieces exactly. There are four raised panels, all fitted into an outer frame.

1. Start by cutting four panels (K) from 1 x 8 pine, each measuring 7 by 14-5/8 inches.

2. Set your saw blade to cut 15 degrees off vertical, and make a 2-inch-long bevel on all four edges of each of the four panels (K). The remaining thickness of the cut side should be 1/8 inch. A diagram of the resulting cut is shown in *Figure 4*.

3. The assembly of the panels within the outer frame is shown in *Figure 5*. To make the frame, rip a total of 13 linear feet of 1 x 4 pine to a width of 2 inches.

4. Cut two side frame pieces (L) from the ripped 1 x 4 pine, each 35-1/2 inches long.

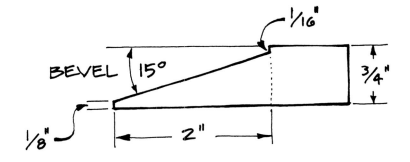

Figure 4

5. Setting each side frame piece (L) on its face, miter both ends at a 45-degree angle as shown in *Figure 5*.

6. Cut two top/bottom frame pieces (M) from the ripped 1 x 4 pine, each 18 inches long.

7. Setting each top/bottom frame piece (M) on its face, miter both ends at a 45-degree angle as shown in *Figure 5*.

8. Cut three inner frame pieces (N) from the ripped 1 x 4 pine, each 14 inches long.

9. The four panels (K) float in a dado that is cut into the frame pieces. Cut a dado 1/4 inch wide and 3/8 inch deep into the shorter edge (which will face toward the center of the finished door) of the top, bottom, and side frame pieces (L and M). (For some assistance in cutting dadoes, refer to the "Tips and Techniques" section.)

10. Cut a dado 1/4-inch wide and 3/8-inch deep into both edges of all three inner frame pieces (N).

11. To make certain that all pieces fit together perfectly, the door should first be assembled without glue or nails. Lay all of the door parts on a level surface. Then, referring to *Figure 5*, place the top frame (M) between the two side frames (L), and match the miters. Set the first panel (K) into the dadoes in the frame pieces (L and M), and fit one inner frame piece (N) between the side frame pieces (L) below the panel. Next, alternately add three more panels (K) and two more inner frame pieces (N). Finally, add the bottom frame piece (M).

12. When you are satisfied that all of the pieces fit correctly, glue and clamp the assembly together and let it sit for a few hours. Glue only the frame pieces together; the

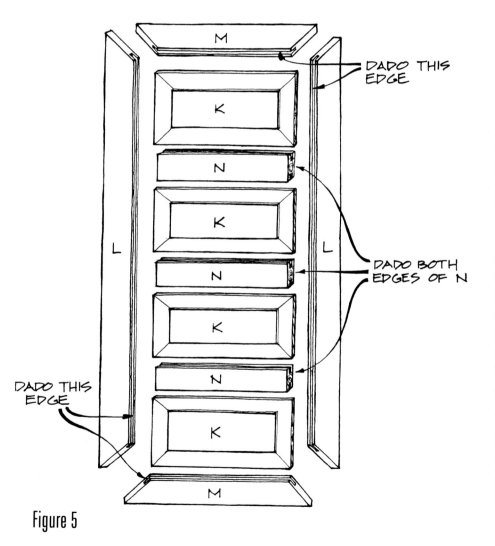

Figure 5

panels should float freely in the dadoes. Reinforce the four corners and each of the inner frame pieces (N) with 8-penny finishing nails.

Hanging the Door

It is easier to hang the door if you first lay the cabinet on its back. Then you will not be supporting the weight of the door while you attempt to hang it.

1. Place the door inside the cabinet and check the fit. It should fit perfectly without binding on the edges. Sand or plane the door if necessary for a perfect fit.

2. Install two hinges on the inside of the cabinet following the manufacturer's directions.

3. Install a door pull on the cabinet door. I used a simple, white ceramic knob.

4. An optional step is to add a magnetic cabinet catch. This is inexpensive, easy to install, and helps keep the door from creeping open.

Finishing

1. Fill any exposed screw and nail holes with wood filler.

2. Sand the completed cabinet.

3. Stain or paint the finished cabinet the color of your choice. I used a dark cherry stain.

ARMOIRE

No house ever has enough storage space, and I built this armoire to satisfy a couple of needs. Inside the armoire is a shelf large enough for the television. Under the shelf are six drawers that can hold a variety of family clutter. (Did I say "clutter?" What I really meant was "treasures"—that's right—family treasures!)

The stylish appearance of this piece belies its easy construction. Although there are a number of steps to follow, each can be accomplished without any advanced woodworking skills. To make an armoire you'll be proud to show your friends, you need only take your time, align the doors and drawers perfectly, and fit the trim molding carefully. No one will guess that you only used the simplest construction techniques.

MATERIALS LIST

Lumber:

18 linear ft. 1 x 2 pine
74 linear ft. 2 x 2 pine
66 linear ft. 1 x 4 pine
42 linear ft. 1 x 8 pine
16 linear ft. 2 x 8 pine
1 pc. 1/4" stain-grade plywood, 4' x 4'
5 sheets 3/4" stain-grade plywood, ea. 4' x 8'
9 linear ft. decorative molding, 3-1/2" wide
9 linear ft. box molding
28 linear ft. 1" x 1" outer corner molding
12 linear ft. fluted molding, 3-1/2" wide
18 linear ft. 1/4" x 1/4" cove molding

Hardware:

6 offset door hinges
2 door levers
6 drawer pulls
2 lbs. #6 x 1-1/4" flathead wood screws
1 lb. #6 x 2" flathead wood screws
2 lbs. #6 x 2-1/4" flathead wood screws
2 lbs. #10 x 3-1/2" flathead wood screws
approx. 100 3d finishing nails
1 small box wire brads

Special Tools and Techniques:

miters
dadoes

CUTTING LIST

Code	Description	Qty.	Material	Dimensions
A	Side	2	3/4" plywood	2' x 6'
B	Inner Vertical Support	4	2 x 2 pine	6' long
C	Back	1	3/4" plywood	4' x 6'
D	Back Horizontal Support	3	2 x 2 pine	43-1/2" long
E	Side Horizontal Support	6	2 x 2 pine	21" long
F	Front Horizontal Support	3	2 x 2 pine	43-1/2" long
G	Top	1	3/4" plywood	43-1/4" x 46-1/2"
H	Bottom	1	3/4" plywood	43-1/4" x 46-1/2"
I	Middle Shelf	1	3/4" plywood	43-1/4" x 46-1/2"
J	Horizontal Side Trim	4	1 x 4 pine	24-3/4" long

(continued on next page)

Code	Description	Qty.	Material	Dimensions
K	Vertical Side Trim	4	1 x 4 pine	65" long
L	Top/Bottom Housing	2	3/4" plywood	21" x 36-1/2"
M	Side Housing	2	3/4" plywood	21" x 37-1/2"
N	Corner Support	4	2 x 2 pine	18-1/4"
O	Housing Back	1	3/4" plywood	36-1/2" x 39"
P	Center Divider	1	3/4" plywood	18-1/4" x 37-1/2"
Q	Center Divider Support	4	2 x 2 pine	18-1/4" long
R	Side Support	2	2 x 2 pine	34-1/2" long
S	Rail	4	1 x 4 pine	35" long
T	Upper Stile	6	1 x 4 pine	7-1/2" long
U	Lower Stile	3	1 x 4 pine	8-1/2" long
V	Drawer Front/Back	8	1 x 8 pine, ripped	11-3/4" long
W	Drawer Side	8	1 x 8 pine, ripped	16" long
X	Drawer Bottom	4	1/4" plywood	11-1/4" x 16-1/2"
Y	Lower Drawer Front/Back	4	1 x 8 pine	11-3/4" long
Z	Lower Drawer Side	4	1 x 8 pine	16" long
AA	Lower Drawer Bottom	2	1/4" plywood	11-1/4" x 16-1/2"
BB	Drawer Panel	4	1/4" plywood	10-1/2" x 5-1/2"
BB2	Lower Drawer Panel	2	1/4" plywood	10-1/2" x 6-1/2"
CC	Drawer-Front Top/Bottom Frame	12	1 x 2 pine	10-1/4" long
DD	Drawer-Front Side Frame	8	1 x 2 pine	5-1/2" long
DD2	Lower Drawer-Front Side Frame	4	1 x 2 pine	6-1/2" long
EE	Vertical Trim	2	1 x 8 pine	6' long
FF	Shelf Trim	1	1 x 4 pine	35" long
GG	Top Trim	1	1 x 4 pine, ripped	35" long
HH	Bottom Trim	1	1 x 4 pine, ripped	35" long
II	Top Side Trim	2	1 x 4 pine	25-1/2" long
JJ	Top Front Trim	1	1 x 4 pine	51" long
KK	Side Molding	2	3-1/2" dec. molding	26-3/4" long
LL	Front Molding	1	3-1/2" dec. molding	52-1/2" long
MM	Side Box Trim	2	box molding	26-1/4" long
NN	Front Box Trim	1	box molding	52" long
OO	Corner Block	4	2 x 8 pine	6" sq.
PP	Front/Back Bas	2	2 x 8 pine	52-1/2" long
QQ	Side Base	2	2 x 8 pine	26-1/4" long
RR	Door	2	3/4" plywood	66" x 17-1/2"
SS	Fluted Trim	2	3-1/2" fluted molding	70" long

Constructing the Armoire Frame

1. Cut two sides (A) from 3/4-inch-thick plywood, each measuring 2 by 6 feet.

2. Cut four inner vertical supports (B) from 2 x 2 pine, each 6 feet long.

3. Attach two supports (B) to one side (A), both flush with the 6-foot edges, as shown in *Figure 1*. Use glue along the entire length, and 2-1/4-inch-long screws approximately every six inches.

4. Repeat step 3 using the remaining side (A) and the two remaining supports (B).

5. Cut one 4-foot by 6-foot back piece (C) from 3/4-inch-thick plywood. Place it on a flat surface and attach the two sides (A) at right angles to the back. Glue and screw the two vertical supports (B) to the back (C) as shown in *Figure 2*. Again, use 2-1/4-inch-long screws about every 6 inches.

Adding the Horizontal Supports

The armoire top, bottom, and the inner shelf are cut from 3/4-inch-thick plywood, and are attached to 2 x 2 pine horizontal supports inside the armoire frame. The horizontal supports fit between the inner vertical supports (B) that you have already attached to the back (C) and sides (A). The back and side horizontal supports should be glued and screwed in place using 2-1/4-inch-long screws placed approximately 6 inches apart.

1. Cut three back horizontal supports (D) from 2 x 2 pine, each 43-1/2 inches long.

2. Attach one back horizontal support (D) flush with the exposed edge of the top of the back (C), between the inner vertical supports (B), as shown in *Figure 3*.

3. Attach a second horizontal support (D) positioned between the two inner vertical supports (B) and flush with the bottom edge of the back (C).

4. Measure 29-1/4 inches from what will be the top of the armoire (it can be either end—now is when you decide), and attach the remaining back horizontal support (D) between the two inner vertical supports, as shown in *Figure 3*.

5. Cut three side horizontal supports (E) from 2 x 2 pine, each 21 inches long.

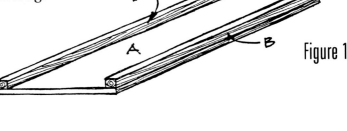

Figure 1

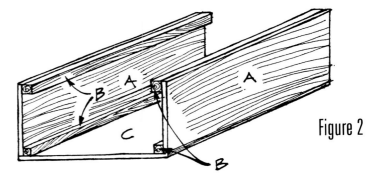

Figure 2

6. Attach one side horizontal support (E) between the inner vertical supports (B) and flush with the exposed top edge of the sides (A), as shown in *Figure 3*.

7. Measure 29-1/4 inches from the top of the armoire, and attach the second side horizontal support (E) between the two inner vertical supports (B), as shown in *Figure 3*.

8. Attach the remaining side horizontal support (E) flush with the bottom exposed edge of the side (A).

9. Repeat steps 5 through 8 to cut and attach three more side horizontal supports (E) to the remaining side (A).

10. Cut three front horizontal supports (F) from 2 x 2 pine, each 43-1/2 inches long.

11. Attach one front horizontal support (F), between the inner vertical supports, at the very top of the sides (A). Use glue and 3-1/2-inch-long screws, screwing through the side (A), through the inner vertical supports (B), and into the end of the front horizontal support (F). See *Figure 4*.

12. Attach the second front horizontal support (F), between the inner vertical supports (B), at the very bottom of the sides (A).

13. Measure 29-1/4 inches from the top of the armoire sides, and attach the remaining front horizontal support (F) between the inner vertical supports (B). Again use glue and 3-1/2-inch long screws.

Adding the Top, Bottom, and Middle Shelf

1. The top (G), bottom (H), and middle shelf (I) are identical. Cut each from 3/4-inch-thick plywood according to the diagram shown in *Figure 5*. Note that a 1-7/8-inch

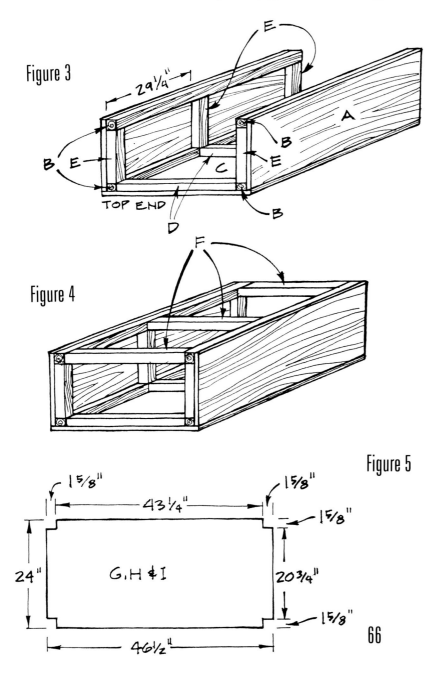

Figure 3

Figure 4

Figure 5

square must be cut from each of the four corners to accommodate the inner vertical supports (B).

2. Stand the armoire (well, half-assembled armoire) right side up. Fit the bottom (H) over the lowest inner 2 x 2 horizontal supports. Glue and screw it to all four of the horizontal supports using 1-1/4-inch-long screws spaced approximately 6 inches apart. Take extra care to make certain that the front horizontal supports (F) are flush with the exposed edges of the bottom (H), as shown in *Figure 6*.

3. Repeat the process to add the middle shelf (I), fitting it onto the horizontal supports that are 29-1/4 inches from the top. Again make sure that the front edges are flush, as you did for the bottom (H).

4. The top (G) is attached to the uppermost horizontal supports, but it is attached on the lower face of those supports so that the horizontal supports will not be visible inside the finished armoire. Attach it in the same manner used for the shelf (I), making sure that the front edges are flush.

Adding the Side Trim

1. Cut two horizontal side trim pieces (J) from 1 x 4 pine, each 24-3/4 inches long. Attach them to the two shorter ends of the sides (A), overlapping the exposed edges of the back (C), as shown in *Figure 7*. Use both glue and 1-1/4-inch-long screws, countersinking the screws.

2. Cut two vertical side trim pieces (K) from 1 x 4 pine, each 65 inches long. Glue and screw them along each of the 6-foot edges of the sides (A), between the horizontal side trim pieces (J), as shown in *Figure 7*. They also cover the exposed edges of the back (C).

3. Repeat steps 1 and 2 to add vertical and horizontal side trim pieces (J and K) to the remaining side (A) of the armoire.

Building the Drawer Housing

The six interior drawers are housed in a plywood box that fits inside the lower portion of the armoire. The completed drawer housing measures 36-1/2 by 39 inches.

Check the dimensions of your assembly at this point to confirm that the completed drawer housing

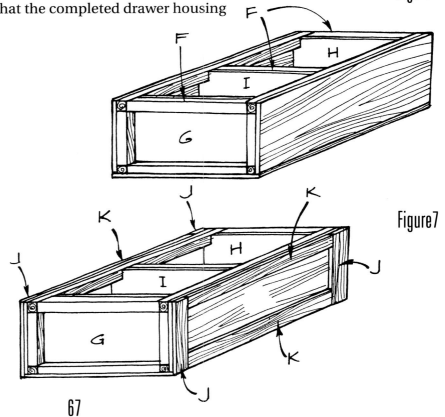

Figure 6

Figure 7

will fit. (It is better to adjust the measurements of the drawer housing now than to discover that it is 1/8 inch too big when you attempt to fit it into the armoire.)

Vertically, the drawer housing fits perfectly between the front horizontal support underneath the middle shelf (I), and the bottom (H), but it is 7 inches less wide than the available horizontal opening. The excess 3-1/2 inches of horizontal space on each side of the drawer housing is needed to accommodate the 1 x 8 trim that you will add later to the front of the armoire. In total, 7-1/4 inches on each side will be covered by the trim.

1. Cut two top/bottom housing pieces (L) from 3/4-inch-thick plywood, each measuring 21 by 36-1/2 inches.

2. Cut two side housing pieces (M) from 3/4-inch-thick plywood, each measuring 21 by 37-1/2 inches.

3. Cut four corner supports (N) from 2 x 2 pine, each 18-1/4 inches long.

4. Glue and screw two of the four corner supports (N) to the 21-inch edges of a side housing piece (M). Use 2-inch-long screws spaced about 6 inches apart. As shown in *Figure 8*, make sure that the corner supports (N) are flush with the back of the drawer housing and 2-3/4 inches short of the front of the housing. This 2-3/4-inch spacing is necessary to accommodate the rails and stiles, which are added later, and to allow space for the drawer fronts and drawer pulls when the armoire doors are closed over the drawer housing.

5. Glue and screw the remaining two corner supports (N) to the remaining side housing piece (M) just as you did in step 4.

6. Place the two side housing pieces (M) between the two top/bottom housing pieces (L). Glue and screw the top/bottom housing pieces (L) to the corner supports (N) at all four corners. You should now have a box measuring 36-1/2 inches wide and 39 inches tall (outside measurements), as shown in *Figure 9*.

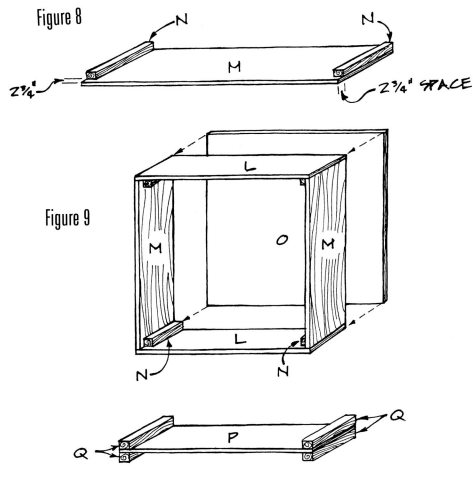

Figure 8

Figure 9

Figure 10

7. Cut one 36-1/2-inch by 39-inch housing back (O) from 3/4-inch plywood.

8. Fit the housing back (O) over the exposed edges of the housing assembly, and glue and screw it in place, as shown in *Figure 9*, using 1-1/4-inch-long screws.

9. Cut one 18-1/4-inch by 37-1/2-inch center divider (P) from 3/4-inch-thick plywood.

10. Cut four center divider supports (Q) from 2 x 2 pine, each 18-1/4 inches long.

11. With 2-inch-long screws, glue and screw all four center divider supports (Q) to both sides of the center divider (P) along the 18-1/4-inch edges, as shown in *Figure 10*.

12. Position the center divider (P) in the exact horizontal center of the drawer housing, flush against the housing back (O), as shown in *Figure 11*. Note that there is a 2-3/4-inch allowance at the front of the drawer housing. Glue and screw the four center divider supports to the housing bottom (L) and housing top (L). Using 2-inch-long screws, screw through the housing back (O) into the ends of the four center divider supports (Q) and into the center divider (P).

13. Cut two side supports (R) from 2 x 2 pine, each 34-1/2 inches long.

14. Glue and screw the two side supports (R) to the housing sides (M), between and flush with the ends of the corner supports (N), 2-3/4 inches from the exposed edges of the housing sides (M). Use 2-inch-long screws, spacing them about 6 inches apart.

Adding the Rails and Stiles

1. The front of the drawer housing consists of rails (horizontal members) and stiles (vertical members). These are the finished front of the drawer housing and also accommodate the drawers. A diagram of the rails and stiles is shown in *Figure 12*. It is very important that all of the stiles and rails are installed exactly square, or your drawers will not fit properly.

2. Cut four rails (S) from 1 x 4 pine, each 35 inches long.

3. Cut six upper stiles (T) from 1 x 4 pine, each 7-1/2 inches long.

4. Cut three lower stiles (U) from 1 x 4 pine, each 8-1/2 inches long.

5. Attach the four rails (S) to the front of the completed housing, paying particular attention to the spacing between them. The four upper openings must be exactly 7-1/2 by 12-1/4 inches, and the lower two openings must be exactly 8-1/2 by 12-1/4 inches, as shown in *Figure 12*. All four of the rails (S) fit inside the exposed edges of the housing sides (M), top (L), and bottom (L). The rails cover the exposed edge of the center divider (P), leaving a 2-inch allowance at the front. Glue and screw them in place with 2-inch-long

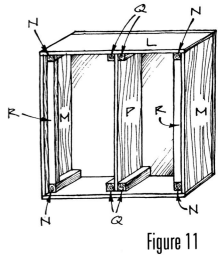

Figure 11

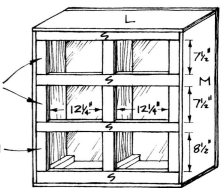

Figure 12

screws, screwing through the rails (S) into the 2 x 2 pine supports.

6. Attach the six upper stiles (T.) as shown in *Figure 12.* They fit flush with the rails and cover the exposed edge of the center divider (P). Glue and screw them in place, screwing through the stiles and into the center divider (P) or side supports (R). Again use 2-inch-long screws. Toenail each of the upper stiles (T) to the adjoining rail (S).

7. Attach the three lower stiles (U) as shown in *Figure 12.* They also fit flush with the rails, and cover the exposed edge of the center divider (P). Glue and screw them in place, screwing through the lower stiles (T) and into the center divider (P) or the side supports (R). Toenail each of them to the rails (S) above and below.

Making the Drawers

There are six drawers that fit into the drawer housing. Although the dimensions of the two bottom drawers differ from those of the

Figure 13

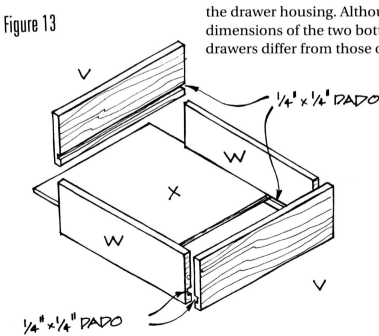

¼" x ¼" DADO

four top drawers, each drawer is constructed identically. An assembly diagram is shown in *Figure 13.*

1. Rip 20 linear feet of 1 x 8 pine to 6-1/2 inches in width.

2. Cut the following pieces from the ripped pine (to construct one of the four upper drawers): two drawer front/back pieces (V), each 11-3/4 inches long, and two drawer sides (W), each 16 inches long.

3. Cut a 1/4-inch by 1/4-inch dado 3/8 inch from the lower edge on the inside of each drawer piece (V and W) to accommodate the plywood bottom. (For some helpful hints on cutting dadoes, refer to the section on "Tips and Techniques.")

4. Cut one 11-1/4-inch by 16-1/2-inch drawer bottom piece (X) from 1/4-inch-thick plywood. Assemble the drawer as shown in *Figure 13* using glue and finishing nails. The decorative drawer front is added later.

5. Repeat steps 2 through 4 three more times to build the additional three upper drawers.

6. Cut the following pieces for one lower drawer from full-width 1 x 8 pine: two lower drawer front/back pieces (Y), each 11-3/4 inches long, and two lower drawer sides (Z), each 16 inches long.

7. Cut a 1/4-inch by 1/4-inch dado 3/8 inch from the lower edge on the inside of each drawer piece (Y and Z) to accommodate the plywood bottom.

8. Cut one 11-1/4-inch by 16-1/2-inch lower drawer bottom piece (AA) from 1/4-inch-thick plywood. Using glue and 3-penny finishing nails, assemble the drawer as shown in *Figure 13*.

9. Repeat steps 6 through 8 to build the additional lower drawer.

Building the Drawer Fronts

Although they have different dimensions, the upper drawer fronts and lower drawer fronts are constructed in exactly the same manner. Each drawer front is nothing more than a center panel of 1/4-inch-thick plywood inserted into a 1 x 2 frame and trimmed with decorative molding (*Figure 14*). It's not difficult to do, but it does require a certain amount of precision when cutting to obtain a professional-looking finished product. For the best results, don't hurry the process, and be meticulous in your work.

1. To make one upper drawer front, cut one 10-1/2-inch by 4-1/2-inch drawer panel (BB) from 1/4-inch-thick plywood.

2. Cut two top/bottom frame pieces (CC) from 1 x 2 pine, each 10-1/4 inches long.

3. Cut two side frame pieces (DD) from 1 x 2 pine, each 5-1/2 inches long.

4. Cut a 1/4-inch by 1/4-inch dado along the center of the inside edges of each of the frame pieces (CC and DD) to accommodate the drawer

panel (BB), as shown in *Figure 14*.

5. Place the drawer panel (BB) into the dadoes cut in the drawer frame pieces (CC and DD). Glue and clamp, then nail the drawer frame pieces (CC and DD) together.

6. Measure and cut four pieces of 1/4-inch cove molding to fit around the inside edges of the frame. Setting each piece of cove molding with the curved side up, miter both ends at a 45-degree angle. Attach the mitered pieces to the drawer frames (CC and DD) with glue and wire brads.

7. Repeat steps 1 through 6 three more times to assemble the remaining upper drawer fronts.

8. The two lower drawer fronts are identical with the upper ones, except that they are 1 inch taller. To construct the two lower drawer fronts, repeat steps 1 through 6 twice more, but with the following modifications: cut the lower drawer panel (BB2) 10-1/2 by 6-1/2 inches (from 1/4-inch-thick plywood); cut each of the two lower drawer-front side frame pieces (DD2) 6-1/2 inches long (from 1 x 2 pine).

Installing the Hardware

1. Follow the manufacturer's instructions to install the metal drawer glide between the housing back (O), and the rails (S).

2. Install a roller on the bottom of each drawer and on the inside of the rail (S), again following the manufacturer's instructions.

Figure 14

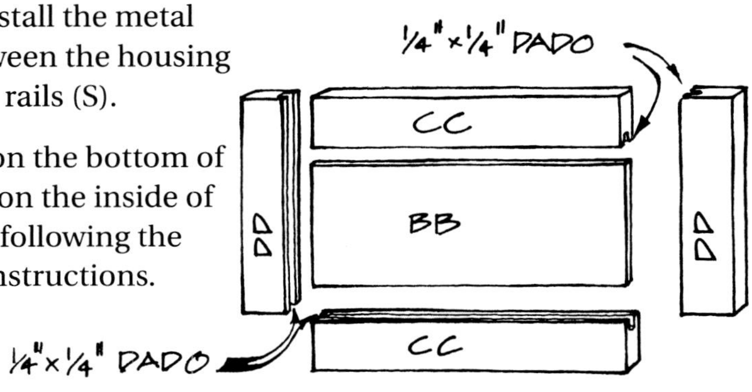

1/4" x 1/4" PADO

CC

BB

DD

DD

CC

1/4" x 1/4" DADO

Attaching the Drawer Fronts

1. For the job to look very professional, each drawer front must be exactly straight and level. Put the assembled drawers inside their respective drawer openings in the cabinet, setting them on the metal drawer glides.

2. Place a scrap piece of wood between the back of the drawer and the back of the drawer housing so that the drawer is held flush with the front of the rails and stiles. Begin with the top-most drawer fronts. Use heavy-duty, double-sided tape to hold the drawer front temporarily in place on the drawer until you have all of the drawer fronts positioned exactly right. Then remove the drawers one at a time, and attach the front to the drawer with two 1-1/4-inch-long screws driven from the inside of each drawer into the drawer-front frame pieces.

Figure 15

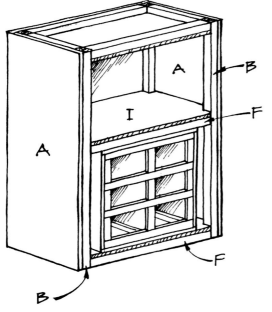

3. Install drawer pulls on each of the drawer fronts.

Attaching the Drawer Housing to the Armoire

1. Slide the completed drawer housing inside the lower section of the armoire. As shown in *Figure 15*, the exposed edges of the drawer housing should be flush with the exposed edges of the middle shelf (I), the front horizontal supports (F), and the bottom (H). The sides of the drawer housing should be positioned equidistant from the vertical supports (B), with 3-1/2 inches of open space on each side of the housing.

2. With 2-1/4-inch-long screws, attach the drawer housing to the armoire, screwing through the top of the housing into the front horizontal support (F). Similarly, screw through the housing bottom into the bottom (H) and into the front horizontal support (F) below the bottom (H). Refer to *Figure 15*.

Adding the Front Trim

1. Cut two vertical front trim pieces (EE) from 1 x 8 pine, each 6 feet long.

2. Attach them on either side of the front of the armoire, over the edges of the side trim pieces (J and K), as shown in *Figure 16*. Use 2-1/4-inch-long screws spaced about 8 inches apart. Place the screws no closer to the outer edges than 3/4 inch.

3. Cut one 35-inch-long shelf trim piece (FF) from 1 x 4 pine.

4. Fit the shelf trim piece (FF) between the two vertical front trim pieces (EE) so that it covers the exposed edge of the middle shelf (I), the front horizontal support (F) below, and the top housing (L). It should be absolutely flush with the top surface of the shelf. Glue and screw it in place using 2-1/4-inch-long screws.

5. Cut one 35-inch-long top trim piece (GG) from 1 x 4 pine. Rip it lengthwise to a width of 2-1/2 inches.

6. Fit the top trim piece (GG) between the two vertical front trim pieces (EE) so that it covers the exposed edge of the top (G) and the front horizontal support (F) above the top (G). Make sure that it is absolutely flush with the bottom surface of the top (G). Glue and screw it in place using 2-1/4-inch-long screws.

7. Cut one 35-inch-long bottom trim piece (HH) from 1 x 4 pine. Rip it lengthwise to a width of 3 inches.

8. Fit the bottom trim piece (HH) between the two vertical front trim pieces (EE) so that it covers the exposed edge of the bottom housing (L), the bottom (H), and the front horizontal support (F) below the bottom (H). With 2-1/4-inch-long screws, glue and screw it in place.

Adding the Top Trim

1. Cut two top side trim pieces (II) from 1 x 4 pine, each 25-1/2 inches long.

2. Glue and screw the top side trim pieces (II) to the top and sides of the armoire, as shown in *Figure 16*, overlapping the horizontal side trim pieces (J) by 1 inch. Use 2-1/4-inch-long screws spaced about 8 inches apart to attach all of the trim pieces to the armoire.

3. Cut one 51-inch-long top front trim piece (JJ) from 1 x 4 pine.

4. Glue and screw the top front trim piece (JJ) to the top front of the armoire, as shown in *Figure 16*,

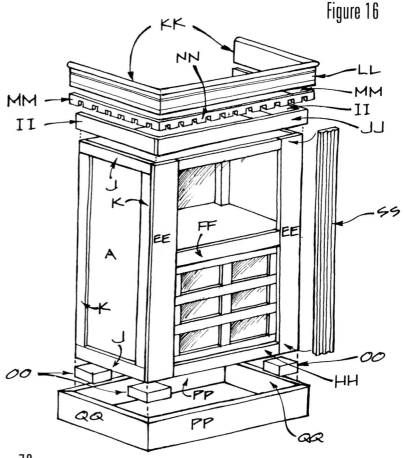

Figure 16

73

overlapping the top trim piece (GG) by 1 inch, and covering the exposed ends of the two top side trim pieces (II).

5. Cut two side molding pieces (KK) from 3-1/2-inch-wide decorative molding, each 26-3/4 inches long.

6. Cut one 52-1/2-inch-long front molding piece (LL) from 3-1/2-inch-wide decorative molding.

7. With each piece standing on edge, miter both ends of the front molding piece (LL) and one end of each of the two side molding pieces (KK) at a 45-degree angle.

8. Glue and nail the three mitered molding pieces to the top of the armoire, as shown in *Figure 16*, overlapping the top front trim (JJ) and the top side trim (II) by 1 inch.

9. Cut two side box trim pieces (MM) from box molding, each 26-1/4 inches long.

10. Glue and nail the box trim pieces (MM) to the top sides of the armoire, just under the side molding pieces (KK), as shown in *Figure 16*.

11. Cut one 52-inch-long front box trim piece (NN) from box molding.

12. Glue and nail the box trim piece (NN) to the top front of the armoire, as shown in *Figure 16*, just under the front molding (LL). The front box trim should cover the exposed ends of the two side box trim pieces (MM).

Adding the Base

The armoire is supported by a 2 x 8 base that is reinforced by blocks at all four corners. The blocks are cut and attached to the armoire first.

1. Cut four corner blocks (OO) from 2 x 8 pine, each 6 inches square.

2. Position them flush with the outermost corners of the bottom of the armoire. Then, using glue and 3-1/2-inch-long screws, screw through the blocks into the 2 x 2 horizontal supports and the 1 x 4 trim pieces at the bottom of the armoire, as shown in *Figure 16*.

3. Cut two front/back base pieces (PP) from the 2 x 8 pine, each 52-1/2 inches long.

4. Stand each front/back base piece (PP) on edge, and miter both ends at a 45-degree angle. Glue and screw the mitered base pieces (PP) in place, overlapping the bottom of the armoire by 1 inch. Screw them securely to the bottom of the armoire and to the corner blocks using 3-1/2-inch-long screws.

5. Cut two side base pieces (QQ) from 2 x 8 pine, each 26-1/4 inches long.

6. Standing the side base pieces (QQ) on edge, miter each end at a 45-degree angle. Glue and screw the side base pieces (QQ) in place, over-lapping the bottom of the armoire by 1 inch and matching the miters on the front/back base pieces (PP). Screw them securely to the bottom

of the armoire and to the corner blocks (OO). Again use 3-1/2-inch-long screws to screw into the corner blocks (OO).

7. Using 3-1/2-inch-long screws, attach the front/back base pieces (PP) to each side base piece (QQ) at the four corners. Insert two screws on each side of all four corners.

Adding the Doors

Before adding the doors, check the measurements of your opening. When placed side by side, the finished doors (with the outer corner molding added) should be 1/2 inch larger than the opening on all four sides.

1. Cut two door pieces (RR) from 3/4-inch-thick plywood, each measuring 17-1/2 by 66 inches.

2. Trim all four sides of the doors (RR) with outer corner molding (be sure to miter the molding at a 45-degree angle on each corner). Attach the molding to the doors with glue and wire brads, counter-sinking the brads.

3. The easiest method to hang the doors is to lay the armoire on its back. Then you will not be supporting the weight of the doors while you attempt to hang them. Place the doors over the opening so that they meet in the center of the opening. Evenly space three hinges underneath each door. Place two hinges the same distance from the top and bottom of each door, and

a third hinge in the center of each door.

4. Follow the manufacturer's directions to attach the hinges to the doors and to the armoire.

5. Attach the door handles to the center of the doors, following the manufacturer's directions.

Installing the Fluted Trim

1. Measure your completed armoire to be certain of the dimensions before cutting the fluted trim for the front sides; the trim should be cut to fit exactly. Then cut two fluted trim pieces (SS) from the 3-1/2-inch-wide fluted molding, each 70 inches long (plus or minus, depending on your measurements).

2. Attach the fluted trim pieces (SS) to the front sides of the armoire, directly over the two vertical front trim pieces (EE), as shown in *Figure 16*. Attach them with glue and 3-penny finishing nails, counter-sinking the nails.

Finishing

1. Fill any nail or screw holes with wood filler.

2. Sand all surfaces thoroughly.

3. Paint or stain the completed armoire the color of your choice.

4. Take an admiring look at your handiwork. It took a lot of effort and time, but what an accomplishment!

CORNER CUPBOARD

Almost everyone has a forgotten and forlorn corner that would benefit from this cupboard. It is only about 14 inches across (at the widest point), but it will hold any number of decorative items that don't seem to fit anywhere else. I've had many compliments on mine—usually followed by, "and if you ever want to build another one, I have just the place for it."

MATERIALS LIST

Lumber:

20 linear ft. 1 x 10 pine
3 linear ft. 1 x 2 pine
28 linear ft. 1 x 4 pine
1 linear ft. 1 x 6 pine
2 linear ft. 3/4"-wide screen molding
4 linear ft. 3-1/2"-wide decorative molding

Hardware:

approx. 100 #6 x 1-1/4" flathead wood screws
approx. 100 6d finishing nails

Special Tools and Techniques:

miters
bevels

CUTTING LIST

Code	Description	Qty.	Material	Dimensions
A	Right Back	1	1 x 10 pine	79" long
B	Left Back	1	1 x 10 pine	79" long
C	Trim	2	ripped from A and B	79" long
D	Back Support	4	1 x 4 pine	79" long
E	Shelf	7	1 x 10 pine	8-1/2" x 8-1/2" x 11-1/4"
F	Middle Shelf Trim	3	1 x 2 pine	11-1/4" long
G	Top Shelf Trim	1	1 x 4 pine	11-1/4" long
H	Bottom Shelf Trim	1	1 x 6 pine, ripped	11-1/4" long
I	Bottom Trim	1	3-1/2" decorative molding	cut to fit (approx. 2' total)
J	Screen Molding	1	3/4" screen molding	cut to fit (approx. 2' total)
K	Top Trim	1	3-1/2" decorative molding	cut to fit (approx. 2' total)

Constructing the Cupboard

1. Cut two 79-inch lengths of 1 x 10 pine and label them right back (A) and left back (B).

2. Rip right back (A) to a width of 8-1/2 inches, cutting off 3/4 inch along its full length. (Refer to *Figure 1*.) This will allow both backs (A and B) to be the same width when they are overlapped and fitted together at the center in a later step.

3. Mark the corners of right back (A) and left back (B) as shown in *Figure 1*

(you'll need the mark for future reference). Then, set your saw blade to cut 45 degrees off vertical, and, as shown in *Figure 1*, rip both the right and left backs lengthwise. Be sure to measure carefully and make your bevel cut exactly 1-1/16 inches from the edge of each back piece (A and B). Save the resulting marked and ripped pieces because they will be re-attached to the same edge to form the trim (C). (That may sound confusing, but it is easy to do. It is explained in a later step.)

4. Attach right back (A) to right back (B), as shown in *Figure 2*, using both glue and screws along the entire joint. Use 1-1/4-inch-long screws evenly spaced about 6 inches apart.

Adding the Shelves

Next you need to add the shelves. This unit has seven shelves—three in the middle, and two each at the top and bottom. The spaces between the upper two shelves and the lower two shelves are covered by trim. The three upper shelf openings are 17 inches high, and the bottom shelf opening measures 17-1/4 inches. Of course, if you want to display shorter items on the shelves, you can increase the number of shelves (and decrease the space between them). Make sure that you space them evenly, adding any "remainder space" to the lowest opening.

1. Measure and cut seven triangular shelf pieces (E) from 1 x 10 pine. Each shelf (E) should measure 8-1/8 inches long on the two sides to match the width of your cupboard backs (A and B). (See *Figure 3*.) As a precautionary measure, check to make sure that both of your cupboard backs (A and B) conform to this width.

2. Measure and mark the placement of all of your shelves (E), following the diagram in *Figure 4*. The top and bottom shelves (E) should be flush with the top and bottom of the cupboard backs (A and B).

3. Check the fit of each triangular shelf (E) in its position before attaching it. Secure the shelves (E) to the cupboard backs (A and B)

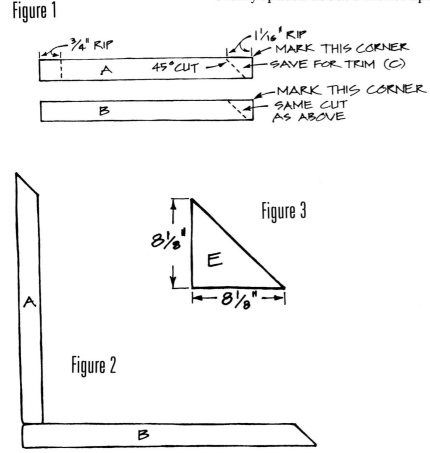

Figure 1

¾" RIP

A   45° CUT

1⅟₁₆" RIP
MARK THIS CORNER
SAVE FOR TRIM (C)

B

MARK THIS CORNER
SAME CUT
AS ABOVE

Figure 3

8⅛"

E

8⅛"

A

Figure 2

B

using both glue and screws. Use six to eight 1-1/4-inch-long screws in each shelf. To prevent the screws from showing in the front, drive them through the cupboard backs (A and B) into the edges of the shelves (C).

4. Turn the trim pieces (C) so that the marked corner and the narrow edge of the trim (C) are in the positions shown in *Figure 5*. Reattach them to the cupboard backs (A and B) using glue and 6-penny finishing nails along the entire length. Space the nails approximately 6 inches apart.

Adding the Back Supports

1. Cut four back support pieces (D) from 1 x 4 pine, each 79 inches long.

2. Attach two back support pieces (D) to the center back of the assembled cupboard, overlapping them as shown in *Figure 5*. Glue and screw the supports (D) to the backs (A and B) using 1-1/4-inch-long screws placed about every 6 inches.

3. Attach the remaining two back support pieces (D) to the outer edges of the cupboard backs (A and B), flush with the re-attached trim (C). Glue and screw them to the cupboard backs (A and B) using 1-1/4-inch-long screws spaced approximately 6 inches apart.

Adding the Shelf Trim

1. Cut three middle shelf trim pieces (F) from the 1 x 2 pine, each

11-1/4 inches long. Attach them to the front of the three middle shelves with glue and 6-penny finishing nails, using about three nails per shelf. Make sure that the top of each shelf trim piece (F) is flush with the top of each shelf (E), as shown in *Figure 5*.

2. Cut one 11-1/4-inch-long top shelf trim piece (G) from 1 x 4 pine. Attach it to the front of the top two shelves (E) with glue and finishing nails, putting three nails into each shelf (E).

3. Rip a 1-foot length of 1 x 6 to a width of 5 inches. Using the resulting 5-inch width, cut one 11-1/4-inch-long bottom shelf trim piece (H).

4. Attach the bottom shelf trim piece (H) between the two bottom shelves (E) using glue and finishing nails. Use three nails across the top and three across the bottom.

Adding the Trim

1. Measure the exact dimensions, as indicated in *Figure 5*, from (1) to (2), from (2) to (3), and from (3) to (4) on the bottom of your cupboard. These are the inside dimensions for your bottom trim pieces (I).

2. From 3-1/2-inch-wide decorative molding, cut three bottom trim pieces (I): two approximately 2 inches long, and one approximately 12-1/2 inches long. Be sure to add a little extra length to each piece to allow for the miters.

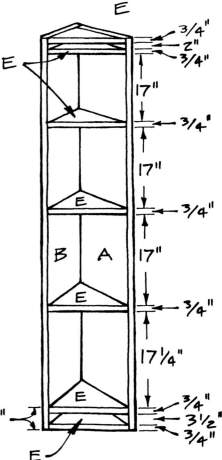

Figure 4

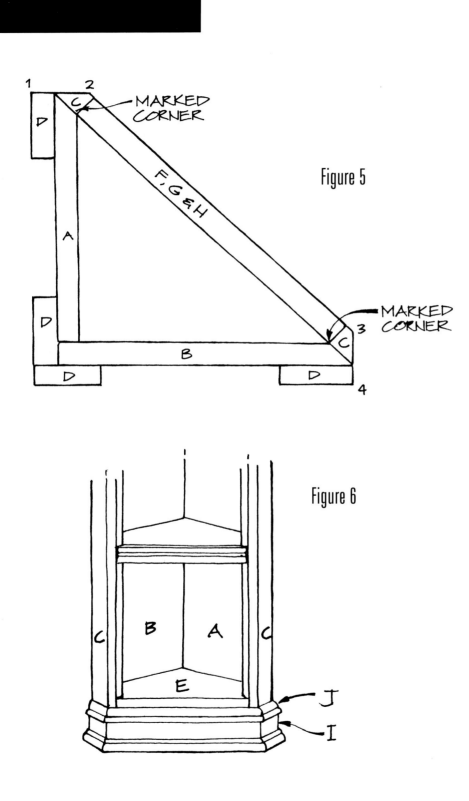

Figure 5

Figure 6

3. Standing each bottom trim piece (I) on its edge, miter one end of each of the shorter lengths and both ends of the longer piece. Set your saw to cut at 22-1/2 degrees, producing an angle of 67-1/2 degrees on the wood.

4. Attach the mitered pieces of molding along the bottom edge of the assembled cupboard, as shown in *Figure 6*. Use glue and 6-penny finishing nails, placing one nail every 3 inches. Countersink all of the nails.

5. Repeat steps 1 through 4, above, using screen molding (J) this time. Attach the cut and mitered strips of screen molding (J) directly above the decorative molding (I), as shown in *Figure 6*, using glue and finishing nails. Space the nails about 3 inches apart and counter-sink them.

6. Repeating the same process, attach 3-1/2-inch-wide decorative molding (K) along the top edge of the assembled cupboard over the shelf trim. Again use glue and finishing nails spaced about 3 inches apart. Countersink the nails.

Finishing

1. Fill any nail holes, cracks, crevices, or knotholes with wood filler, and sand the entire cupboard.

2. Paint or stain the cupboard the color of your choice.

KITCHEN CABINET

Does anyone ever have enough kitchen cabinets? Here is one you can build for your kitchen with just a modest knowledge of woodworking techniques. It contains two good-sized drawers above, extra storage space below, and a wooden counter top. Place it against a wall, or use it as a free-standing island. The finished cabinet is 25 inches deep, 37 inches wide, and 37-1/2 inches tall.

This project is a little more advanced than many of the others and requires you to make several dadoes. You can avoid some of the dadoes, by purchasing pre-made cabinet doors and drawer fronts. Step-by-step instructions for the doors and drawer fronts are included if you want to make them yourself.

Photo: Preston Poe

KITCHEN CABINET

MATERIALS LIST

Lumber:

1 sheet 3/4" plywood, 4' x 8'*
1/2 sheet 3/4" plywood, 4' x 4'*
1 pc. 1/4" clear plywood, 2' x 2'
41 linear ft. 1 x 4 pine*
5 linear ft. 1 x 1 pine
1 pc. laminated 1 x 4 pine, 24" x 36"
(OR 21 linear ft. 1 x 4 pine)
2 drawer fronts, 5" x 13-1/2"
2 cabinet doors, 23-1/2" x 13-1/2"
(OR, to make your own doors and drawer fronts:
  16 linear ft. 1 x 2 pine*
  4 sq. ft. 1/4" plywood*
  16 linear ft. decorative molding, 1/2" wide x 1/4" thick)

Hardware:

1 lb. 3d finishing nails
small wire brads
4 cabinet door hinges*
2 sets of drawer guides and rollers
2 drawer pulls

Special Tools and Techniques:

web clamp
2 or 3 bar clamps (optional)
dadoes
miters

See "Notes on the Materials," below.

CUTTING LIST

Code	Description	Qty.	Material	Dimensions
A	Cabinet Side	2	3/4" plywood	23-1/2" x 36-3/4"
B	Cabinet Back	1	3/4" plywood	34" x 36-3/4"
C	Cabinet Shelf	2	3/4" plywood	23" x 34-1/2"
D	Back Support	1	1 x 4 pine	34" long
E	Top Rail	1	1 x 4 pine	35-1/2" long
F	Side Stile	2	1 x 4 pine	30-1/4" long
G	Center Rail	1	1 x 4 pine	28-1/2" long
H	Upper Center Stile	1	1 x 4 pine	4" long
I	Lower Center Stile	1	1 x 4 pine	22-3/4" long
J	Bottom Base	1	1 x 4 pine, ripped	35-1/2" long
K	Shelf Trim	4	1 x 1 pine	12-1/2" long
L	Cabinet Top	1	laminated pine	23-1/2" x 35-1/2"
M	Long Top Trim	2	1 x 4 pine, ripped	37" long
N	Short Top Trim	2	1 x 4 pine, ripped	25" long
O	Drawer Front/Back	4	1 x 4 pine	12"long
P	Drawer Side	4	1 x 4 pine	20" long
Q	Drawer Bottom	2	1/4" plywood	11" x 20"

Code	Description	Qty.	Material	Dimensions
Q	Drawer Bottom	2	1/4" plywood	11" x 20"
R	Drawer Panel	2	1/4" plywood	10-1/2" x 2"
S	Drawer Top/ Bottom Frame	4	1 x 2 pine	10" long
T	Drawer Side Frame	4	1 x 2 pine	5" long
R2	Cabinet Panel	2	1/4" plywood	10-1/2" x 21"
S2	Cabinet Top/ Bottom Frame	4	1 x 2 pine	10" long
T2	Cabinet Side Frame	4	1 x 2 pine	21" long

Notes on the Materials

If you want a natural finish on your cabinet, you need to buy stain-grade plywood, which is more expensive. Otherwise, purchase paint-grade material for all of the plywood specified. If you opt for stain-grade plywood, make sure to choose wood with a matching grain for all of the parts specified in pine in this materials list.

The top of the cabinet is constructed of laminated 1 x 4 boards. Most building-supply stores sell sections of pine that have already been laminated. If you want to laminate the boards yourself, you need 21 linear feet of 1 x 4 pine and at least two bar clamps.

To attach the doors, I used a decorative semi-concealed hinge. The visible side is attached to the cabinet and the concealed side is attached to the back of the cabinet door. Other styles are also available.

Constructing the Cabinet Frame

1. Cut two cabinet sides (A) from 3/4-inch-thick plywood according to the dimensions given in *Figure 1*.

2. Cut one cabinet back (B) from 3/4-inch-thick plywood according to the dimensions given in *Figure 2*.

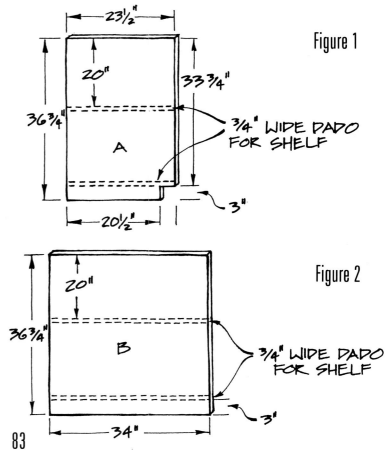

Figure 1

Figure 2

3. Cut two cabinet shelves (C) from 3/4-inch-thick plywood, each measuring 23 by 34-1/2 inches.

4. Inspect each face of the two cabinet sides (A), and choose the better ones to face outward on the finished cabinet. On the inner faces of the two cabinet sides (A) and the cabinet back (B), cut two dados, each 3/4-inch-wide and 1/4-inch deep, at the heights indicated in *Figures 1* and *2*. These provide support for the shelves (C).

5. Assemble the two sides (A), back (B), and two shelves (C), as shown in *Figure 3*. Note that the shelves (C) slide into the dadoes. Check to make sure that all of the parts are square and level. Use glue and 3-penny finishing nails spaced about 6 inches apart to secure the pieces together, and fasten a web clamp around the assembly for added strength. Leave the cabinet clamped overnight. (If you are unsure about how to use clamps for this assembly, consult "Tips and Techniques.")

6. Cut one 34-inch-long back support (D) from 1 x 4 pine. Measure and draw a line 4 inches down from the top across the cabinet back (B). Nail and glue the back support (D) to both sides (A) and to the back (B). Place one nail about every 6 inches. This strengthens the cabinet and is used later to brace the metal drawer glides that support the drawers.

Adding the Rails and Stiles

1. The front of the cabinet consists of rails (horizontal members) and stiles (vertical members). These members fulfill two functions: they support the cabinet doors, and they form the finished front. A diagram of their placement is shown in *Figure 4*. It is very important that you install each of the stiles and rails so that they are all exactly square, or your drawers and cabinet doors will not fit properly.

2. Cut one 35-1/2-inch-long top rail (E) from 1 x 4 pine. Using glue and two finishing nails on each end, attach the top rail (E) flush with the top edges of the cabinet sides (A), as shown in *Figure 4*.

3. Cut two side stiles (F) from 1 x 4 pine, each 30-1/4 inches long, and attach them to the cabinet sides (A) below the top rail (E). Use glue and 3-penny finishing nails, spacing the nails about 6 inches apart. As shown in *Figure 4*, the stiles should be flush with the outer edges.

Figure 3

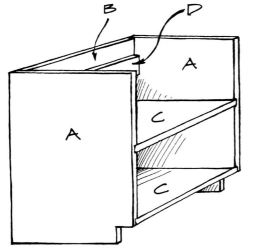

4. Cut one 28-1/2-inch-long center rail (G) from 1 x 4 pine, and attach it 4 inches below the top rail (E), between the two side stiles (F). After applying glue, toenail the center rail (G) into the side stiles (F) using two finishing nails on each end.

5. From 1 x 4 pine, cut one 4-inch-long upper center stile (H) and one 22-3/4-inch-long lower center stile (I).

6. Attach the upper center stile (H) between the top rail (E) and the center rail (G), as shown in *Figure 4*. Apply glue, and toenail the center stile (H) into the top rail (E) and the center rail (G), placing two finishing nails at each end. The lower center stile (I) is attached to each of the shelves (C). Make certain that both of the shelves (C) are perfectly level in the center. Use glue and two finishing nails to attach the lower center stile (I) to each of the shelves (C). Glue and toenail the lower center stile (I) to the center rail (G).

7. Cut a 35-1/2-inch length of 1 x 4 pine. Rip the length to 3 inches in width, and attach the resulting bottom base piece (J) across the bottom edge of the assembled cabinet so that it covers the raw, bottom edges of the cabinet sides (A), as shown in *Figure 4*. To secure the attachment, first glue all of the exposed joints. Then use two 3-penny finishing nails to toenail the bottom base piece (J) to the lower center stile (H). Next, with two finishing nails on each end, attach the bottom base piece (J) to the edges of the cabinet sides (A). Finally, nail through the lower

cabinet shelf (C) into the bottom base piece with finishing nails placed about 6 inches apart.

8. Cut four shelf trim pieces (K) from 1 x 1 pine, each 12-1/2 inches long. Use glue and finishing nails placed every 6 inches to attach the shelf trim (K) to the exposed fronts of each of the shelves (C) between the stiles (F and I).

Making the Top

1. If you purchased material already laminated, trim the piece to 23-1/2 by 35-1/2 inches to make the cabinet top (L). Then skip down to step 4.

2. To do the lamination yourself, cut seven lengths of 1 x 4 pine, each 35-1/2 inches long. Before gluing the wood lengths together, it is a good idea to rip a minuscule amount

Figure 4

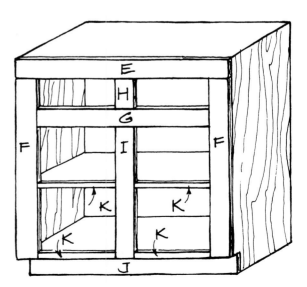

from each edge to ensure a solid bond in the lamination process. Then spread glue on the adjoining edges, and place the lengths of wood side by side. Clamp them together securely, using at least two bar clamps, and leave them clamped overnight.

3. Trim the completed top (L) to 23-1/2 by 35-1/2 inches by ripping 1/2 inch from each 35-1/2-inch-long edge.

4. Set the top (L) onto the cabinet assembly flush with all four of the cabinet's outer edges. Use glue and finishing nails, placing the nails about every 6 inches, to attach the top (L) to the cabinet.

5. Rip 11 feet of 1 x 4 pine to a width of 2 inches. The resulting material is used to trim the cabinet top (L).

6. From the 2-inch material, cut two long top trim pieces (M), each 37 inches long, and two short top trim pieces (N), each 25 inches long.

7. Setting each piece on its 2-inch face, miter both ends of all four top trim pieces (M and N) at a 45-degree angle. Glue and nail the short trim pieces (N) to the edges of the laminated cabinet top (L) using 3-penny finishing nails spaced about 6 inches apart.

8. Glue and nail the long trim pieces (M) to the front and back of the laminated cabinet top (L). Use finishing nails placed about every 6 inches, and countersink all of the nails.

Making the Drawers

There are two identical drawers in this cabinet. Both are constructed as shown in the assembly diagram in *Figure 5*.

1. Cut the following parts for the drawer from 1 x 4 pine: two drawer front/back pieces (O), each 12 inches long, and two drawer sides (P), each 20 inches long.

2. Cut a 1/4-inch by 1/4-inch dado on the inside of each drawer piece (O and P), 3/8 inch from the lower edge, to accommodate the plywood bottom.

3. Cut one 11-inch by 20-inch drawer bottom (Q) from 1/4-inch-thick plywood. Assemble the drawer as shown in *Figure 5*. Use glue and finishing nails, placing two nails on each end of the overlapping boards. The drawer front is added later.

4. Repeat Steps 1 through 3 to build the second drawer.

Figure 5

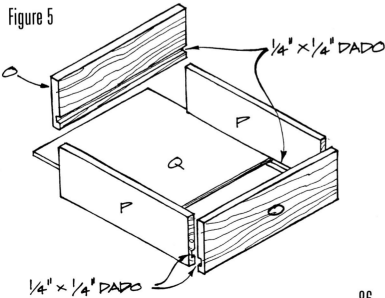

1/4" x 1/4" DADO

1/4" x 1/4" DADO

Making the Drawer Fronts

If you purchased your drawer fronts and cabinet doors, skip down to "Installing the Hardware," below. These instructions describe how to make your own, starting with the construction of the drawer fronts. Although they have different dimensions, the drawer fronts and cabinet doors are built in exactly the same manner.

The drawer front is nothing more than a center panel of 1/4-inch plywood that is inserted into a 1 x 2 frame, and trimmed with decorative molding (*Figure F*). It's not difficult to do, but it requires a certain amount of precision when cutting to obtain a professional-looking finished product. Don't hurry the process, and be meticulous in your work.

1. Cut one 10-1/2-inch by 2-inch drawer panel (R) from 1/4-inch-thick plywood.

2. Cut two drawer top/bottom frame pieces (S) from 1 x 2 pine, each 10 inches long.

3. Cut two drawer side frame pieces (T) from 1 x 2 pine, each 5 inches long.

4. Cut a 1/4-inch by 1/4-inch dado along the inside edges of each of the frame pieces (S and T) to accommodate the drawer panel (R). A cutting diagram is shown in *Figure 6*.

5. Place the drawer panel (R) into the dadoes cut into the frame pieces (S and T). Glue and clamp, then nail the frame pieces together. Use two 3-penny finishing nails on each end of the overlapping boards.

6. Allowing a little extra length for the miters, cut four pieces of 1/4-inch-thick decorative molding to fit around the inside edges of the frame. Set the molding so that the decorative edge faces up, and miter both ends of each piece at a 45-degree angle. Attach the mitered pieces to the plywood panel with glue and wire brads. Countersink the brads.

7. Repeat Steps 1 through 6 to assemble the second drawer front.

Making the Cabinet Doors

1. The cabinet doors are constructed using the same procedures that you followed for the drawer fronts. The only difference is the size of the parts. To make one cabinet door, cut one 10-1/2-inch by 21-inch panel (R2) from 1/4-inch-thick plywood.

2. Cut two cabinet top/bottom frame pieces (S2) from 1 x 2 pine, each 10 inches long.

Figure 6

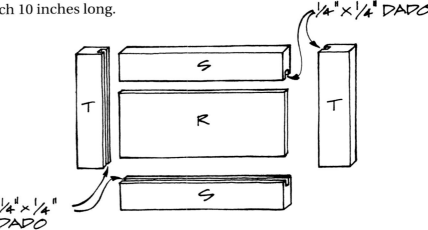

1/4" x 1/4" DADO

1/4" x 1/4" DADO

3. Cut two cabinet side frame pieces (T2) from 1 x 2 pine, each 21 inches long.

4. To construct the cabinet doors, follow steps 1 through 7 (substituting R2, S2, and T2 for R, S, and T) in the previous section, "Making the Drawer Fronts."

Installing the Hardware

1. Follow the manufacturer's instructions to install the metal drawer glide between the back support (D), and the center rail (G).

2. Install a roller on the bottom of each drawer, and on the inside of the center rail (G), again following the manufacturer's instructions.

Installing the Doors and Drawer Fronts

1. The easiest method is to attach the drawer fronts first. For the job to look very professional, all of the drawers and doors must be exactly straight and level. Set the assembled drawers inside the drawer opening in the cabinet, placing them on the metal drawer glides. Place a scrap piece of wood between the back of each drawer and the back of the cabinet so that the drawers are held flush with the front of the cabinet. Use heavy-duty, double-sided tape to hold a drawer front temporarily in place on each drawer until you have both drawer fronts positioned exactly right. Then attach the fronts to the drawers. Use two finishing nails driven from the inside of

the drawer into the drawer top frame (S), and two finishing nails driven into the drawer bottom frame (S).

2. Measure carefully, and install the hinges on each of the doors. The hinges should be positioned the same distance from the top and bottom of each door.

3. Have someone help you support the doors, and hold the doors with the attached hinges over the door opening. Line up each door so that its width is exactly even with the width of the drawer above it, and make sure both doors are at an even height with each other. Then screw the remaining sides of the hinges to the cabinet.

4. Attach the drawer pulls on each of the drawers and on the cabinet doors. The pulls should be evenly spaced and aligned with one another.

Finishing

1. Countersink all of the nails, and fill the resulting holes with wood filler.

2. Sand every surface thoroughly.

3. Paint or stain the completed cabinet the color of your choice. For the cabinet in the photograph, I stained the laminated top and painted the remainder of the cabinet white.

4. To customize your cabinet, you can add wood molding at the base to match the existing molding in your kitchen. If the cabinet is to be a freestanding island, you may wish to add base molding on all four sides.

MATERIALS LIST

Lumber:

1 pc. laminated 1 x 4 pine, 20" sq.
(OR 11 linear ft. 1 x 4 pine)
24 linear ft. 1 x 4 pine
18 linear ft. 2 x 2 pine
7 linear ft. 1 x 2 pine

Hardware:

approx. 100 #6 x 1-1/4" flathead wood screws
approx. 100 #6 x 2" flathead wood screws
4 casters*

Special Tools and Techniques:

2 or 3 bar clamps (optional)

See "Notes on the Materials," below.

CUTTING LIST

Code	Description	Qty.	Material	Dimensions
A	Top	1	laminated pine	20" sq.
B	Short Frame	2	1 x 4 pine	20" long
C	Long Frame	2	1 x 4 pine	21-1/2" long
D	Leg	4	2 x 2 pine	34" long
E	Leg Reinforcement	4	2 x 2 pine	17" long
F	Shelf Support	4	1 x 2 pine	20" long
G	Shelf Slat	10	1 x 4 pine	20" long

UTILITY CART

Before building this cart, I had planned to keep it in my kitchen to store over-sized bowls, pans, and appliances. Now that it is finished, I have found lots of other uses for it. I move it outdoors to use as a mobile potting bench; indoors it works as a portable bar when we have parties, and in the laundry room it houses my laundry basket and makes a good table for folding clothes just out of the dryer. I may have to build several more!

Notes on the Materials

When you select casters for this project, make certain that the ones you choose can hold the weight of whatever you want to store on the cart. They must also be small enough to be installed on the bottom of legs cut from 2 x 2 pine.

The top of the utility cart is constructed of laminated 1 x 4 pine boards. Most building-supply stores sell sections of pine that have already been laminated. Otherwise, if you want to laminate the boards yourself, you need approximately 11 linear feet of 1 x 4 pine and at least two heavy-duty bar clamps.

Laminating the Top

1. If you purchased pine that is already laminated, simply cut one piece, 20 inches square, and proceed to "Framing the Top," below.

2. To make the laminated top (A),

UTILITY CART

cut six lengths of 1 x 4 pine, each 20 inches long. (Together these add up to only 10 linear feet, but you must purchase a little extra length to make up for the material lost with each saw cut.)

To ensure a solid bond in the lamination process, it is a good idea to rip a minuscule amount from each edge to be laminated before gluing the wood lengths together. Place the lengths of wood side by side, and spread glue on the edges to be joined. Clamp the pieces together securely using at least two bar clamps, and leave them overnight.

3. Trim the completed top (A) to 20 inches square.

Framing the Top

1. The top (A) is simply a 20-inch-square section of laminated pine that is framed by 1 x 4 pine boards. Cut two short frame pieces (B) from 1 x 4 pine, each 20 inches long.

2. Glue and screw the two short frame pieces (B) to opposite edges of the laminated square top (A), as shown in *Figure 1*. The edges of the short frame pieces (B) should be flush with the top surface of the laminated square top (A). Use 1-1/4-inch-long screws, and space them about four inches apart. Countersink the screws.

3. Cut two long frame pieces (C) from 1 x 4 pine, each 21-1/2 inches long.

4. Glue and screw the two long frame pieces (C) to the remaining two edges of the laminated square top (A), as shown in *Figure 1*. The long frame pieces (C) cover the exposed ends of the short frame pieces (B). Again use glue and 1-1/4-inch-long screws placed about every four inches. Countersink the screws.

Adding the Legs

1. Cut four legs (D) from 2 x 2 pine, each 34 inches long.

2. Turn the laminated top (A) with its attached frame pieces (B and C) upside down on a level surface. Glue and screw one leg (D) in each of the four inside corners of the top, as shown in *Figure 2*. Screw through

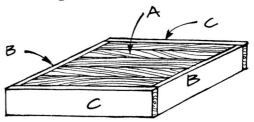

Figure 1

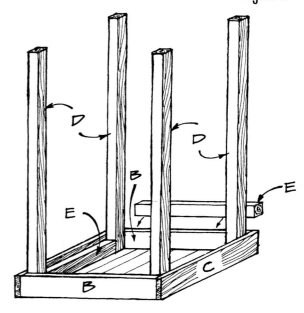

Figure 2

the face of each frame piece (B and C) into the leg (D) using two 2-inch-long screws at each end. The legs are a little wobbly at this point, but they will be reinforced in the next step.

3. Cut four leg reinforcements (E) from 2 x 2 pine, each 17 inches long.

4. Fit each leg reinforcement (E) between one pair of legs, making sure that each is flush against the top (A) and the frame pieces (B and C). Glue and screw them in place. Use 2-inch-long screws, and space them about 4 inches apart. Screw through the leg reinforcements (E) and into both the top (A) and the frame pieces (B and C).

Adding the Shelf Supports

1. Cut four shelf supports (F) from 1 x 2 pine, each 20 inches long.

2. With the assembly still upside down, measure 1-1/4 inches down from the ends of two adjacent legs (any two). Attach one shelf support (F) on the inside, connecting those two legs, as shown in *Figure 3*. Use glue and one 2-inch-long screw on each end of the shelf support (F).

3. Next measure 17 inches from the same ends of the same two legs. Glue and screw a second shelf support (F) on the inside of those two legs at the 17-inch mark *(Figure 3)*.

4. Repeat steps 2 and 3 to attach the remaining two shelf supports (F) to the insides of the remaining two legs.

Adding the Shelf Slats

1. Each shelf is composed of five 1 x 4 pine slats that are held in place by the shelf supports (F).

2. Cut five shelf slats (G) from 1 x 4 pine, each 20 inches long.

3. The two outermost slats of the shelf must be notched to accommodate the legs. Using the cutting diagram shown in *Figure 4* as a guide, notch two of the five shelf slats (G).

4. Turn the assembly right side up. Place the five shelf slats so that

Figure 3

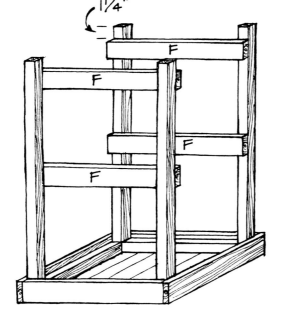

they are supported by the lower two shelf supports (F). The notches cut into the two outer shelf slats (G) should fit around the legs, as shown in *Figure 5*. Space the remaining three shelf slats (G) evenly across the length of the shelf supports (F).

Glue and screw the shelf slats (G) to the shelf supports (F). Use 1-1/4-inch-long screws, and place two screws at each end of each middle slat, and one at each end of each outer slat. I left the screws showing as a decorative accent, but you can countersink the screws and fill the holes if you wish.

5. Repeat steps 2 through 4 to complete the second shelf.

Finishing

1. Fill all screw holes with wood filler.

2. Sand the completed project thoroughly.

3. Finish with the stain or paint of your choice. I painted the legs white and finished the rest of the project with a maple-colored stain.

4. Set the cart upside down on a clean surface (to prevent the top from getting marred). Then, following the manufacturer's instructions, install the casters on the bottom of the legs.

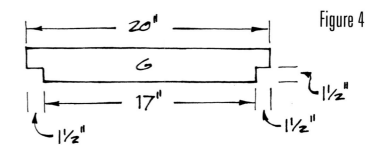

Figure 4

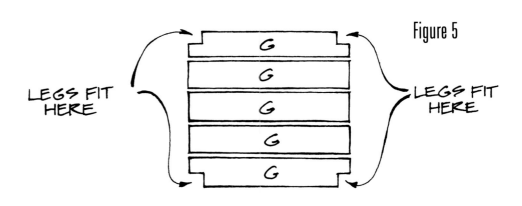

Figure 5

Outdoor Living

MATERIALS LIST

Lumber:

3 pcs. laminated 1 x 4 pine:
    2 pcs. 14" x 36"
    1 pc. 16" x 46-1/2"
(OR 44 linear ft. 1 x 4 pine)
25 linear ft. 1 x 4 pine
13 linear ft. 1 x 6 pine

Hardware:

approx. 100 #6 x 1-1/4" flathead wood screws
approx. 50 #6 x 2-1/4" flathead wood screws

Special Tools and Techniques:

2 or 3 heavy-duty bar clamps (optional)

CUTTING LIST

Code	Description	Qty.	Materials	Dimensions
A	Side	2	laminated pine	14" x 36"
B	Vertical Back	8	1 x 6 pine	19" long
C	Horizontal Back	4	1 x 4 pine	45" long
D	Seat	1	laminated pine	16" x 46-1/2"
E	Seat Support	2	1 x 4 pine	13-1/4" long
F	Center Support	1	1 x 4 pine	43-1/2" long
G	Front Support	1	1 x 4 pine	45" long

COUNTRY BENCH

This handsome, sturdy bench can be used either inside or out-of-doors. It would be attractive in an entry hall, on a front or back porch, or even in a child's room. I painted mine a bright red to match my entry door, but it would also be pretty with a stain finish or if left natural with just a wood sealer applied. The finished bench is 46-1/2 inches wide, 36 inches tall, and 16 inches deep.

Notes on the Materials

Both the sides and the seat of this bench are constructed from laminated 1 x 4 pine boards. Most building-supply stores sell sections of pine that have already been laminated. If you want to laminate the boards yourself, you need 44 linear feet of 1 x 4 pine and at least two heavy-duty bar clamps.

Making the Bench Sides

1. If you purchased pine that is already laminated, simply cut two pieces, each 14 by 36 inches, making two sides (A). Then skip down to step 4.

2. If you want to laminate the boards yourself, cut four lengths from 1 x 4 pine, each 36 inches long. To ensure a solid bond in the lamination process, it is a good idea to rip a minuscule amount from each

(Enlarge by 600% to get actual size.)

Figure 1

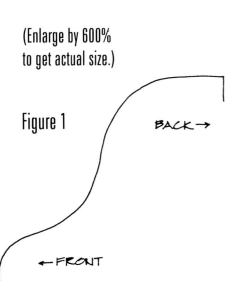

BACK→

←FRONT

(Enlarge by 600% to get actual size.)

Figure 2

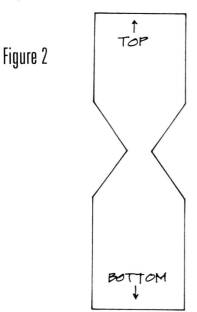

↑
TOP

BOTTOM
↓

edge to be joined before gluing the wood lengths together. Place the boards side by side, and wipe glue on the adjoining 36-inch-long edges. Then clamp the four boards together using at least two bar clamps. (Refer to the "Tips and Techniques" section if you need assistance with clamping procedures.) Leave the assembly clamped for at least 24 hours. You now have one side (A) measuring 14 by 36 inches.

3. Repeat step 2 to laminate the second side (A).

4. The top edge of each side (A) is then cut in a curve according to the pattern shown in *Figure 1*. Enlarge the pattern and trace it onto the top of both laminated sides, Then, following the pattern lines, cut the curves.

Making the Back

The back of the bench consists of eight lengths of 1 x 6 pine that are set side by side vertically and sandwiched—top and bottom—between two horizontal 1 x 4 pine boards.

1. Cut eight vertical back pieces (B) from 1 x 6 pine, each 19 inches long.

2. *Figure 2* shows the decorative pattern that is cut in each vertical back piece (B). Enlarge the pattern, trace it onto one of the vertical back pieces (B), and cut the board along the pattern lines. Use the resulting cut board to mark the same pattern on each of the remaining seven ver-

tical back pieces (B).

Be sure to use the first board you cut as the pattern for each subsequent back piece so that the resulting cuts will all be the same.

3. Sand each of the vertical back pieces (B) now because it will be difficult to sand them after the back is assembled.

4. Cut four horizontal back pieces (C) from 1 x 4 pine, each 45 inches long.

5. Set two of the horizontal back pieces (C) on a level work surface, placing them parallel to each other and with the inside edges 12 inches apart.

6. Lay the eight vertical back pieces (B) evenly spaced on top of the horizontal back pieces (C). As shown in *Figure 3*, the ends of the verticals (B) should be flush with the outer edges of the horizontals (C).

7. Attach the vertical back pieces (B) to the two horizontals (C) using glue and 1-1/4-inch-long screws. One screw in each end of each of the verticals (B) should be sufficient.

8. Place the remaining two horizontal back pieces (C) on top of the assembly, making sure to align them with the horizontals already attached. As shown in *Figure 4*, the verticals (B) are now sandwiched between the horizontals (C). Glue and screw the two unattached horizontal back pieces in place using

eight 1-1/4-inch-long screws for each horizontal board. Place one screw over the center of each end of each of the verticals (B).

Making the Seat

1. If you purchased pine that is already laminated, simply cut one piece 16 by 46-1/2 inches, making the seat (D). Then skip down to step 4.

2. If you want to laminate the boards yourself, cut five pieces from 1 x 4 pine, each 46-1/2 inches long. Rip a minuscule amount from each edge to be joined, and place the boards side by side. Wipe glue on the adjoining edges, and clamp the five boards together using at least two bar clamps. Leave the assembly clamped for a minimum of 24 hours.

3. Rip one edge of the laminated assembly to make the overall width 16 inches. You now have one seat (D) measuring 16 by 46-1/2 inches.

4. Next, as shown in *Figure 5*, cut a notch 3/4 inch deep and 14 inches long on each end of the seat (D). To provide the most support, position the 46-1/2-inch-long front of the seat on the edge that still retains a full-width board (the non-ripped edge).

Attaching the Seat

1. Cut one 13-1/4-inch-long seat support (E) from 1 x 4 pine.

2. Measure 16 inches from the bottom of one side (A), and attach the seat support (E) as shown in *Figure 6*. It should fit flush at the back edge and 3/4 inch from the front edge of the side (A). Use glue and four or five 1-1/4-inch screws, screwing through the seat support (E) into the side (A).

3. Repeat steps 1 and 2 to cut and attach a second seat support (E) to the remaining side (A). The seat supports (E) are both on the inside of the bench, so make certain that the two sides (A) with seat supports (E) attached are mirror images of each other.

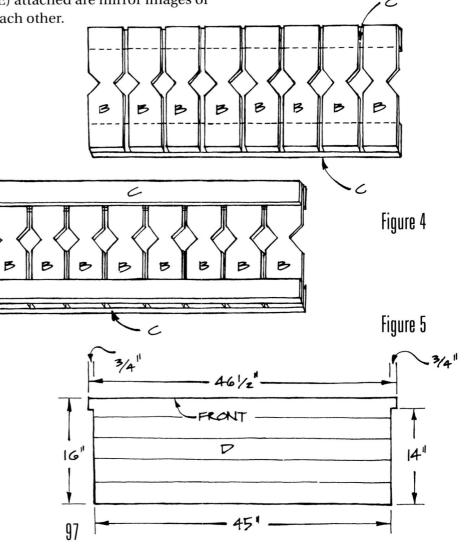

Figure 3

Figure 4

Figure 5

97

4. Cut one 43-1/2-inch-long center support (F) from 1 x 4 pine.

5. This next step will require some assistance from a couple of helpers. (If assistants are not available, use bar clamps to help with this assembly.) Place the two side assemblies so that the attached seat supports (E) are facing each other. As shown in *Figure 7*, place the center support (F) between the two seat supports (E), 4 inches from what will be the back of the completed bench. Use glue and two 2-1/4-inch-long screws on each end of the center support (F). Screw through the side assembly, through the seat support (E), and into the center support (F). Don't worry if the result is rather wobbly at this point. It will be reinforced in the next step.

6. Cut one 45-inch-long front support (G) from 1 x 4 pine. Position it across the front of the bench and attach it to the exposed ends of the seat supports (E). Use glue and two 1-1/4-inch-long screws at each end of the front support (G).

7. Place the seat (D) on top of the seat supports (E), center support (F), and front support (G). Note that the longer 46-1/2-inch edge fits across the front, and that it overlaps the sides (A), as shown in *Figure 8*. Glue and screw the seat in place using 1-1/4-inch-long screws. Screw through the seat (D) into the supports (E, F, and G), placing one screw about every 4 or 5 inches. Countersink all of the screws.

Adding the Back

1. Carefully fit the back assembly between the two sides (A). As shown in *Figure 8*, the back assembly should fit flush with the top of both of the sides.

2. Glue and screw the back assembly in place. Screw through each side (A) into the back assembly, using three or four 2-1/4-inch-long screws at both the top and bottom. Countersink the screws.

Finishing

1. Fill any exposed screw holes with wood filler.

2. Sand the completed bench.

3. Stain or paint the finished bench in the color of your choice. If you plan to use it outside, be sure to use exterior-grade finishing materials.

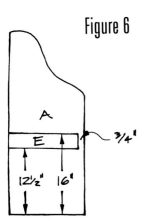

Figure 6

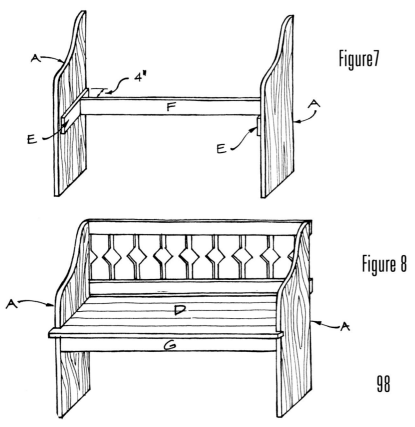

Figure 7

Figure 8

This perky bench really lightens the mood on my front porch; it nearly always brings a smile to the faces of those who ring my doorbell. This bench is not difficult to make, and it provides handy seating on the porch— perfect for watching some of the crazy antics of your neighbors. The finished bench is 34 inches wide, 35 inches tall, and 20-1/2 inches deep.

PORCH BENCH

PORCH BENCH

MATERIALS LIST

Lumber:

26 linear ft. 1 x 4 pine
18 linear ft. 1 x 2 pine
7 linear ft. 2 x 4 pine
5 linear ft. 1 x 10 pine

Hardware:

approx. 100 #6 x 1-1/2" flathead wood screws
approx. 20 #6 x 2-1/2" flathead wood screws

CUTTING LIST

Code	Description	Qty.	Material	Dimensions
A	Half Leg	4	1 x 10 pine	14-1/2" long
B	Leg Support	4	2 x 4 pine	19-3/4" long
C	Bottom Support	1	1 x 4 pine	29-3/4" long
D	Wide Slat	3	1 x 4 pine	34" long
E	Narrow Slat	3	1 x 2 pine	34" long
F	Wide Back Slat	3	1 x 4 pine	34" long
G	Narrow Back Slat	3	1 x 2 pine	34" long
H	Back Support	2	1 x 4 pine	35" long

Notes on the Materials

If you plan to put the finished bench in an unprotected area on your porch, make certain that all of your screws are galvanized, and that you seal the completed project with a protective coat of exterior paint and sealer.

Making the Legs

1. Each leg assembly is constructed from two lengths of 1 x 10 material supported on the top and bottom by 2 x 4s. Cut two half legs (A) from 1 x 10 pine, each 14-1/2 inches long.

2. A pattern for the heart cutout is provided in *Figure 1*. Enlarge and trace the pattern onto the center of one edge of the half leg (A), as shown in *Figure 2*, and cut along the traced line. Save the resulting half heart (that was a halfhearted cut, right?) for later. Repeat the process for the other half leg.

3. Cut two leg supports (B) from 2 x 4 pine, each 19-3/4 inches long.

4. Stand the two legs (A) on edge with the cutouts facing each other. Center both legs on the face of one leg support (B). The two legs should be positioned 1/4 inch apart and 1/2 inch from each end of the leg support (B), as shown in *Figure 3*.

Screw through the leg support (B) into the edge of each leg (A) using about five 2-1/2-inch-long screws. Attach the remaining leg support (B) to the other end of the two legs (A).

5. Repeat steps 1 through 4 to construct the second leg assembly.

Building the Seat

1. Cut one 29-3/4-inch-long bottom support (C) from 1 x 4 pine.

2. As illustrated in *Figure 4*, center the bottom support (C) between the two leg assemblies. Apply glue, then screw the bottom support (C) to the top of the lower leg supports (B) using at least two 1-1/2-inch-long screws on each end.

3. Cut three wide slats (D) from 1 x 4 pine, each 34 inches long.

4. Cut three narrow slats (E) from 1 x 2 pine, each 34 inches long.

5. Glue and screw one narrow slat (E) to the tops of both upper leg supports (B), making it flush with the front ends and side edges, as shown in *Figure 4*. Use 1-1/2-inch screws, and place the screws 1-1/2 inches from the ends of the slats. (The results look nicer if you draw a line across each of the slats at the 1-1/2-inch mark and put all of your screws on the line.) I used one screw on each end of the narrow slats (E), and two screws on each end of the wide slats (D).

6. Add the remaining pieces, alternating wide slats (D) and narrow

slats (E), and space them a little less than 1 inch apart *(see Figure 4)*. The outermost slats should be flush with both the ends and the side edges of the upper leg supports (B).

Adding the Back

1. Cut three wide back slats (F) from 1 x 4 pine, each 34 inches long.

2. Cut three narrow back slats (G) from 1 x 2 pine, each 34 inches long.

3. Cut two back supports (H) from 1 x 4 pine, each 35 inches long.

4. The back is assembled in the same manner as the seat, alternating wide and narrow slats, and leaving about an inch between the slats. Again, place the screws 1-1/2 inch from the ends of the slats. Use two 1-1/2-inch-long screws on each end of the wide slats, and one screw on each end of the narrow slats. Begin by attaching one wide back slat (F) flush with the ends of both back supports (H), as shown in *Figure 5*.

5. Continue to add slats, alternating narrow back slats (G) and wide back slats (F), to complete the seat-back assembly.

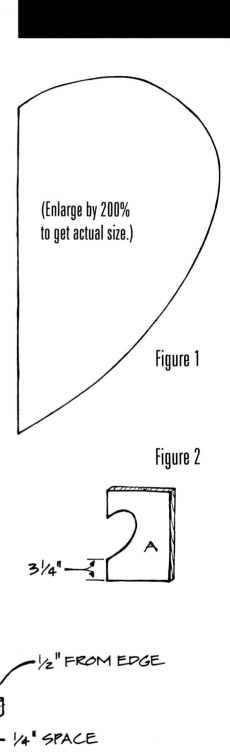

(Enlarge by 200% to get actual size.)

Figure 1

Figure 2

3/4"   A

1/2" FROM EDGE

1/4" SPACE

1/2"

B   A   A   B

Figure 3

6. Glue and screw the seat-back assembly to the assembled seat, screwing through the back supports (H) into the ends of the two leg supports (B). Use 2-1/2-inch-long screws, placing two screws into the end of each leg support (B).

Finishing

1. Fill any holes, cracks, and crevices with wood filler, and thoroughly sand the completed bench.

2. Paint or stain the completed bench the color of your choice.

3. Now you need the half-heart cutouts that you have faithfully saved. Paint or stain the cutouts in a contrasting color, and let them dry. I got a little festive with my paint choices. I painted the bench white, let the paint dry, then dribbled light green paint on top. I painted the cutouts solid green.

4. Position the painted cutouts on the seat back as shown in the picture. The exact measurements are not important; make any arrangement you like. Use glue and two or three 1-1/2-inch-long screws to attach the cutouts to the back assembly.

5. Place the finished bench on your porch and watch for the smiles.

Figure 4

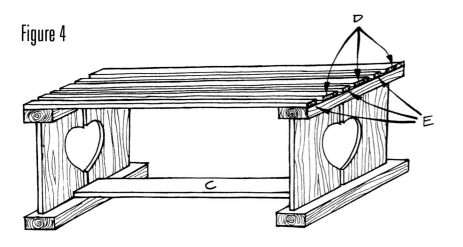

Figure 5

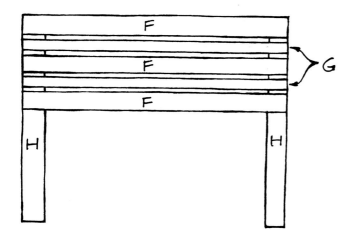

If you cook outside, you've probably had the same frustrations that we've had. When you reach the grill carrying the tray of food, barbecue tools, special sauce, and seasonings, there is no place to put it. This barbecue surround solves the problem admirably.

I designed this surround to fit my husband's "irreplaceable" old smoker and grill. You can copy this design exactly, or alter it to fit your own grill. The directions include methods for making modifications.

BARBECUE SURROUND

BARBECUE SURROUND

MATERIALS LIST

Lumber:

20 linear ft. 2 x 4 treated lumber*
6 linear ft. 4 x 4 treated lumber*
32 linear ft. 1 x 4 treated lumber*
9 linear ft. 3-1/2" fluted trim
2 pcs. from scrap, ea. 1/4" x 1" x 3-1/2" (optional)

Hardware:

approx. 75 #6 x 2-1/2" flathead galvanized wood screws
approx. 50 #12 x 4-1/2" flathead galvanized wood screws
approx. 50 2d galvanized finishing nails
approx. 100 3d galvanized finishing nails

Special Tools and Techniques:

miters (optional)

See "Notes on the Materials," below.

CUTTING LIST

Code	Description	Qty.	Material	Dimensions
A	Long Side	2	2 x 4 treated lumber	30" long
B	Short Side	1	2 x 4 treated lumber	12-1/2" long
C	Long Back	1	2 x 4 treated lumber	37-1/2" long
D	Short Back	1	2 x 4 treated lumber	14" long
E	Front	1	2 x 4 treated lumber	54-1/2" long
F	Leg	4	4 x 4 treated lumber	17-1/4" long
G	Long Leg Support	1	2 x 4 treated lumber	28-1/2" long
H	Short Leg Support	1	2 x 4 treated lumber	12-1/2" long
I	Support Block	4	2 x 4 treated lumber	3-1/2" long
J	Long Table Slat	5	1 x 4 treated lumber	56-1/2" long
K	Short Table Slat	5	1 x 4 treated lumber	18" long
L	Trim	3	3-1/2" fluted trim	cut to fit (approx. 9' total)
M	Corner Stop (optional)	2	scrap treated lumber	1/4" x 1" x 3-1/2"

Notes on the Materials

The above materials are sufficient to make the barbecue surround pictured. If you modify the design, you will also need to alter the materials list.

Because the surround will be used outdoors, make certain that you use only exterior-grade materials, including your adhesives and fasteners.

Confirming the Design

1. If you want to build the surround exactly as pictured, skip down to "Building the Frame." To modify the design, you must first determine the size of your grill. Measure the width, depth, and height, and note any obstructions that need to be cleared by the finished surround.

2. The easiest way to modify the design is to draw it out on paper. The first step is to draw the dimensions of the frame. The surround should be flush with the grill on the inside, and the top surface should be at least 15 inches wide (enough to accommodate a large platter).

3. The next step is to decide how tall you want your surround. Measure from the ground to where you want the top surface. Subtract 3/4 inch (to accommodate the top slats), and you have the length of your legs.

4. Total the amount of each of the materials needed for your design, and alter your materials list accordingly. Also, to help you plan your purchases, adjust the cutting list as needed.

5. Read all of the directions below to make certain that you understand them thoroughly. This will enable you to make slight adjustments in the procedures as you build your own unique barbecue surround.

Building the Frame

1. A diagram of the assembled frame is shown in *Figure 1*. Refer to this when cutting the following parts from 2 x 4 treated lumber:

Code	Description	Qty.	Length
A	Long Side	2	30 inches
B	Short Side	1	12-1/2 inches
C	Long Back	1	37-1/2 inches
D	Short Back	1	14 inches
E	Front	1	54-1/2 inches

2. Place the frame pieces on a level surface in the arrangement shown in *Figure 1*. Begin by attaching the two long sides (A) to the front (E). Screw through the front (E) into the ends of the long sides (A). Each joint should be glued and secured with at least two 2-1/2-inch-long screws.

3. Attach the short side (B) to the front (E). Screw through the front (E) into the end of the short side (B).

4. Fit the short back (D) between the two long sides (A). Secure it in place by screwing through the long sides (A) into the ends of the short back (D).

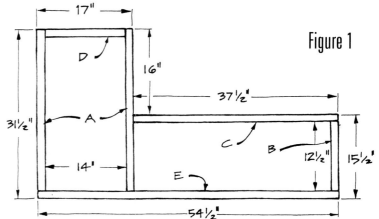

Figure 1

5. Attach one end of the long back (C) over the exposed end of the short side (B). Screw through the long back (C) into the end of the short side (B).

6. Measure and mark the point on the inner long side (A) that is 16 inches from the end attached to the short back (D).

7. Secure the unattached end of the long back (C) to the long side (A) at the mark. Screw through the long side (A) into the end of the long back (C).

Attaching the Legs

1. Cut four legs (F) from 4 x 4 treated lumber, each 17-1/4 inches long.

2. Place the frame assembly on a level surface. Fit the four legs (F) in each of the outer corners, as shown in *Figure 2*. Glue and screw them in place on two sides with 4-1/2-inch-

long screws. Use three screws through the frame on two sides of each leg.

3. From 2 x 4 treated lumber, cut one long leg support (G) measuring 28-1/2 inches long.

4. Glue and screw the long leg support (G) to the two legs (F) between the short back (D) and the front (E), as shown in *Figure 3*. Use two 2-1/2-inch-long screws each through the short back (D) and the front (E) into the ends of the long leg support (G). Use two 4-1/2-inch-long screws through the long leg support (G) into each of the two legs (F).

5. Cut one 12-1/2-inch-long short leg support (H) from 2 x 4 treated lumber.

6. Glue and screw the short leg support (H) to the remaining two legs (F) between the long back (C) and the front (E), as shown in *Figure 3*. Use two 2-1/2-inch-long screws each through the long back (C) and the front (E) into the ends of the short leg support (H). Use two 4-1/2-inch-long screws through the short leg support (H) into each of the two legs (F).

7. Cut four support blocks (I) from 2 x 4 treated lumber, each 3-1/2 inches long.

8. Fit one support block (I) against the back leg, between the long leg support (G) and the long side (A), as shown in *Figure 3*. Glue and screw it in place using two 2-1/2-inch-long screws through the long

Figure 2

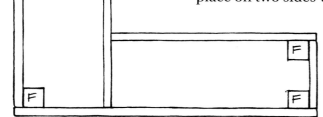

Figure 3

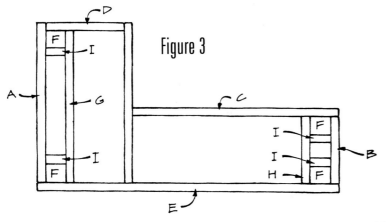

side (A), and two 2-1/2-inch-long screws through the long leg support (G) into the ends of the support block (I). Insert two 4-1/2-inch-long screws through the support block (I) into the leg (F).

9. One at a time, fit the remaining three support blocks (I) against the other three legs. As you did in step 8, glue and screw the support blocks in place using 2-1/2-inch-long screws through the sides (A and B) and leg supports (G and H) into the ends of the support blocks (I). Insert 4-1/2-inch-long screws through the support blocks (I) into the legs (F).

Adding the Table Slats

1. Cut five long table slats (J) from 1 x 4 treated lumber, each 56-1/2 inches long.

2. Refer to *Figure 4* to guide your placement of the table slats. Glue and nail one long table slat (J) into the outermost position across the front of the frame so that it overhangs the frame by 1 inch on the front and on each side. Drive two 3-penny finishing nails through the long table slat (J) into the short side (B), and two nails through the long table slat (J) into each of the long sides (A).

3. Glue and nail three more long table slats (J) to the frame, placing the nails as you did in step 2. Position each new slat directly next to the previously attached one, and make sure that all of the ends are even.

4. Place (do not glue or nail) the remaining long table slat (J) in the innermost position, next to the four attached slats. Use a pencil to mark the bottom of the slat where it overhangs the frame (refer to *Figure 4*).

5. Cut off the portion of the long table slat (J) that overhangs the frame. The slats need to be flush with the frame so that the surround will stand right up next to your grill.

6. Replace the long table slat (J), and glue and nail it to the frame in the same manner that you used for the four previous slats.

7. Cut five short table slats (K) from 1 x 4 treated lumber, each 18 inches long.

8. Attach four of the short table slats (K) to the frame over the two long sides (A). The short table slats (K) should be flush with the inner long side (A), and overhang the outer long side (A) by 1 inch, as shown in *Figure 4*. Use glue and drive two 3-penny finishing nails through each short table slat (K) into each of the long sides (A).

Figure 4

(Diagonal lines indicate portion of slats to be cut away. Dotted lines indicate placement of frame beneath slats.)

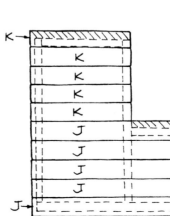

9. Place (do not glue or nail) the last short table slat (K) behind the four previously attached slats. Use a pencil to mark the bottom of the short table slat (K) where it overhangs the frame (refer to *Figure 4*).

10. Because I wanted to be able to put my surround (and grill) up against a wall, I cut off the entire portion of the short table slat (K) that overhangs the frame. If you wish, you can cut the short table slat (K) so that it overextends by 1 inch to match the overhang on the front and sides.

11. Replace the short table slat (K),and attach it to the frame with glue and finishing nails just as you did for the four previous slats.

Adding the Trim

The front and sides of the surround are trimmed with 3-1/2-inch-wide fluted wood molding (L). Rather than mitering the trim, I angled the corners using small corner stops (M). These are pieces 1 inch wide, 3-1/2 inches long, and 1/4 inch thick that I cut from scrap lumber. You can miter your trim or use the stops, whichever you prefer.

1. Measure and cut three pieces of fluted trim: one for the front, and one for each of the sides. The exact length will vary depending upon whether or not you wish to miter your corners.

2. If you want to miter the corners, stand the trim pieces on edge, and miter both ends at a 45-degree angle.

3. Nail and glue the three trim pieces to the front and sides of the frame. Use glue and 2-penny finishing nails placed about every 6 inches.

4. If you did not miter the trim pieces, cut two corner stops (M) from scrap treated lumber, each measuring 1 inch wide, 3-1/2 inches long, and 1/4 inch thick. Use glue and 2-penny finishing nails to attach the pieces to the two front corners. Be sure to drill pilot holes before nailing into these small pieces.

Finishing

1. Countersink all of the nails, and fill them with wood filler.

2. Thoroughly sand the finished project.

3. Stain or paint the surround the color of your choice. I used a maple-colored exterior stain.

4. Place the surround around your barbecue grill, grab some steaks, and start cooking!

The finished size of this cocktail table is 36 inches wide, 24 inches deep, and 18 inches tall. It is perfect for a wide variety of purposes. We use ours out on the patio. It's large enough to hold a plate of hors d'oeuvres and drinks, or a whole tray of snacks.

TILED COCKTAIL TABLE

TILED COCKTAIL TABLE

MATERIALS LIST

Lumber:

16 linear ft. 2 x 4 treated lumber*
11 linear ft. 1 x 4 treated lumber*
1 pc. 3/4" exterior-grade plywood, 22-1/2" x 34-1/2"

Hardware:

approx. 100 #6 x 1-1/4" galvanized flathead wood screws
approx. 50 #6 x 2-1/2" galvanized flathead wood screws

Tiles and Supplies:

tile to cover 22-1/2" x 34-1/2" area*
tile grout (small container)
tile mastic (small container)
tile sealer (small bottle)

Special Tools and Techniques:

trowel
rubber-surfaced trowel
tile cutter (if necessary)*
miters

See "Notes on the Materials," below.

CUTTING LIST

Code	Description	Qty.	Material	Dimensions
A	Long Frame	2	2 x 4 treated lumber	27-1/2" long
B	Leg	4	2 x 4 treated lumber	17" long
C	Corner Support	4	2 x 4 treated lumber	6" long
D	Short Frame	2	2 x 4 treated lumber	19-1/2" long
E	Top	1	3/4" exterior-grade plywood	22-1/2" x 34-1/2"
F	Long Trim	2	1 x 4 treated lumber	36" long
G	Short Trim	2	1 x 4 treated lumber	24" long

Notes on the Materials

Pressure-treated lumber, exterior-grade plywood, and galvanized screws have been specified for this project since it was built to use outdoors. You could substitute redwood or any other wood suitable for exterior use. If you intend to keep the table inside, an interior wood such as pine would be fine. Make certain that you use the appropriate adhesive and fasteners (either exterior or interior).

When choosing the tile for this table, consider that you must cover an area measuring 22-1/2 by 34-1/2 inches. If the tile you choose will not fit into these dimensions evenly, you can either alter the dimensions of the table or cut some of the tiles.

To install the tiles, you need a trowel for spreading the mastic and a rubber-surfaced trowel for applying the grout. If you opt to trim the tile to fit the table dimensions, you also need a tile cutter.

Building the Frame

1. From 2 x 4 treated lumber, cut two long frame pieces (A), each 27-1/2 inches long, four legs (B), each 17 inches long, and four corner supports (C), each 6 inches long.

2. To make a leg assembly, place one long frame (A) between two legs (B), as shown in *Figure 1*. The cut ends of the two legs (B) should be flush with one edge of the long frame (A). Use glue and screws to attach a corner support (C) to both the long frame (A) and the leg (B) to reinforce the joint. As shown in *Figure 1*, the corner support should be 1-1/2 inches from the outer edge of the leg (B). Use two 2-1/2-inch-long screws on each end of each corner support (C).

3. Repeat step 2 to make a second leg assembly using the remaining long frame (A), two legs (B), and two corner supports (C).

4. Cut two short frames (D) from 2 x 4 treated lumber, each 19-1/2 inches long.

5. Place the two leg assemblies on a flat surface so that the corner supports face each other, as shown in *Figure 2*. Place the two short frames (D) between the leg assemblies. Glue and screw through the leg assemblies into the ends of the short frames (D) using two 2-1/2-inch-long screws on each joint.

Adding the Top and Trim

1. Cut one 22-1/2-inch by 34-1/2-inch top (E) from 3/4-inch-thick plywood.

2. Glue and screw the top (E) onto the table frame assembly. Use 1-1/4-inch-long screws placed about every 4 inches around the entire perimeter of the top (E). Screw through the top (E) into the long frame (A), legs (B), and short frames (D). Countersink all of the screws.

3. Cut two long trim pieces (F) from 1 x 4 treated lumber, each 36 inches long.

4. Standing the long trim pieces (F) on edge, miter both ends of each piece at a 45-degree angle.

5. Cut two short trim pieces (G) from 1 x 4 treated lumber, each 24 inches long.

6. Again set the trim on edge, and miter both ends of each short trim piece (G) at a 45-degree angle.

7. The four trim pieces are attached to the frame just a "hair" higher than 1/4 inch above the top (E). The standard tile thickness is 1/4 inch,

Figure 1

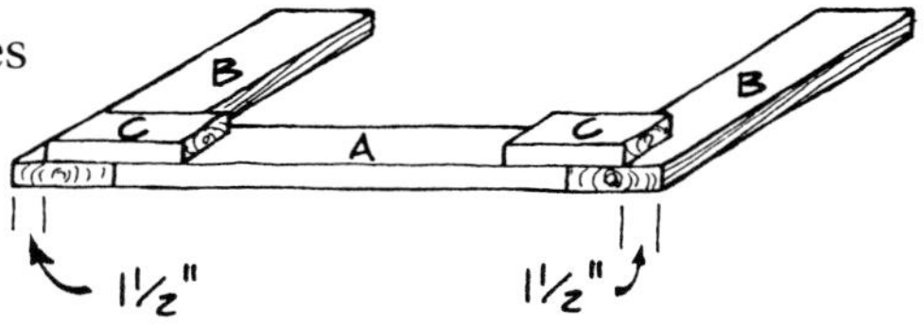

Figure 2

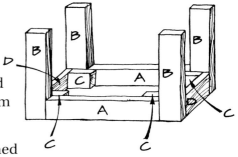

and the "hair" more is to accommo-date the thickness of the tile mastic. *Figure 3* shows the placement of the trim pieces (F and G).

Center one long trim piece (F) lengthwise over one of the long frames (A) so that the mitered ends of the trim (F) extend evenly beyond the ends of the frame (A). Remember to put the long trim piece (F) so that it is just a hair more than 1/4 inch above the ply-wood top. Use glue and three or four 1-1/4-inch-long screws to anchor the long trim (F) in place.

8. Next, position one short trim piece (G) so that one mitered end matches that of the long trim piece (F) already attached. Glue and screw the short trim (G) to the short frame (D) underneath it using two or three 1-1/4-inch-long screws.

9. Repeat steps 7 and 8 to attach the remaining long and short trim pieces (F and G) to the frame.

Adding the Tile

1. Following the manufacturer's directions carefully, spread an even coat of tile mastic over the surface of the top (E) with a trowel.

2. Place the tiles on the mastic one at a time, making sure that they are absolutely straight. Do not slide them, or the mastic will be forced up on the sides of the tile. Let the mastic dry overnight.

3. Mix the tile grout according to the manufacturer's directions (or use pre-mixed grout).

4. Spread the grout over the tile using a rubber-surfaced trowel. Work in an arc, and hold the trowel at an angle so that the grout is forced evenly into the spaces between the tiles.

5. When the grout begins to set up, use a damp rag to wipe the excess off from the tiles and the joints. If you let it dry, the hardened grout will be very difficult to remove. The idea is to use as little water as possi-ble when removing the excess so that you don't thin the grout that remains. Let the grout dry overnight.

6. Rinse the remaining film from the tile and wipe it with an old towel.

7. Apply grout sealer, following the manufacturer's directions.

Finishing

1. Fill any screw holes with wood filler.

2. Thoroughly sand all of the wood parts on the completed table.

3. Stain or paint the wood portions of the table the color of your choice. I used a maple-colored exterior stain.

Figure 3

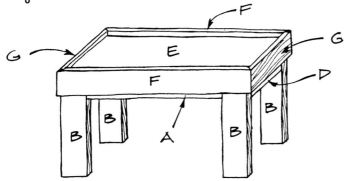

For years we had a patio table that could only be described as pathetic. Every year we dragged it out, sprayed it with six cans of black paint, and put it back on the deck. Then we spent the rest of the summer griping about how spindly it was, and that we should have replaced it. This year we finally did. Our new table is sturdy enough to withstand children, large dogs, and Texas winds, and it is handsome enough to invite compliments.

The finished table is 37 inches square and 27-1/2 inches high. If you plan to leave your table where it will be unprotected from the elements, be sure to use waterproof glue for all assemblies.

PATIO TABLE

PATIO TABLE

MATERIALS LIST

Lumber:

9 linear ft. 4 x 4 treated lumber
10 linear ft. 2 x 4 treated lumber
35 linear ft. 2 x 6 treated lumber
3 linear ft. 2 x 2 treated lumber
(or rip your own 2 x 2 from wider material)

Hardware:

approx. 50 #10 x 3" galvanized flathead wood screws
approx. 50 #12 x 4-1/2" galvanized flathead wood screws
approx. 50 8d galvanized finishing nails

Special Tools and Techniques:

miters

CUTTING LIST

Figure 1

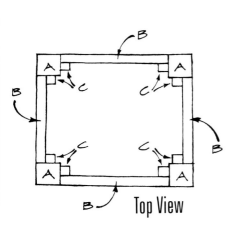

Side View

Top View

Code	Description	Qty.	Material	Dimensions
A	Leg	4	4 x 4 treated lumber	26" long
B	Side Support	4	2 x 4 treated lumber	27" long
C	Support Block	8	2 x 2 treated lumber	3-1/2" long
D	Table Trim	4	2 x 6 treated lumber	37" long
E	Slat	10	2 x 6 treated lumber	cut to fit

Constructing the Base

1. Cut four legs (A) from 4 x 4 treated lumber, each 26 inches long.

2. Cut four side supports (B) from 2 x 4 treated lumber, each 27 inches long.

3. Cut eight support blocks (C) from 2 x 2 treated lumber (or wider material ripped to 2 x 2), each 3-1/2 inches long.

4. The base consists of four legs (A) connected by four side supports (B). Because the finished base must be absolutely straight, its assembly should be done on a level surface. It is also easier to assemble upside down (not you—the table).

Refer to *Figure 1* and attach the side supports (B) to the legs (A). Drive 4-1/2-inch-long screws at an angle (toenail) through the top and bottom of each side support (B) into each leg (A). Countersink the screws. Make sure that the side supports (B) are flush with the top end and the outer surfaces of each Leg (A). Reinforce each joint by attaching a support block (C) to both sides of each Leg (A) and to the adjoining side supports (B).

Use two 3-inch-long screws on each side of each support block (C). This assembly is further reinforced by the table trim pieces in the next step, so don't panic if the table seems less than perfectly stable at this stage.

5. Cut four table trim pieces (D) from 2 x 6 treated pine, each 37 inches long.

6. Standing each table trim piece (D) on its edge, miter both ends at a 45-degree angle. Attach the mitered trim to the assembled base 1-1/2 inches above the side supports (B), as shown in *Figure 2*. Use exterior wood glue and 4-1/2-inch-long screws to attach the trim pieces to the legs (A). Use at least three screws on each end of each table trim piece (D).

Constructing the Table Top

The table top consists of 2 x 6 slats that are mitered at a 45-degree angle on both ends and placed diagonally inside the table trim pieces (D). They are supported by the side supports (B) and the legs (A).

Figure 3 shows the placement of each of the slats. The slats are numbered in the diagram to indicate the order in which they are attached.

1. Setting the first slat on its face, miter one end at a 45-degree angle. Then place the slat so that its long edge fits diagonally across the center of the table top. Mark the length

and miter the remaining end of the first slat (E).

2. Continue to cut and miter the nine remaining slats (E), working out to the corners. The last slat (E) in each corner is actually just a small triangle.

3. When all of the slats (E) have been positioned, nail each of them in place, countersinking the nails. Use at least two 8-penny galvanized finishing nails on each end of each slat (E).

Finishing

1. Fill all of the nail holes, and any cracks and crevices with exterior-grade wood filler. Then sand every surface.

2. Stain or paint the completed table the color of your choice using exterior-grade finishing materials.

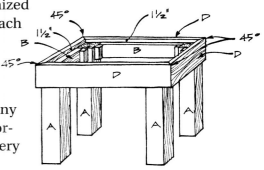

Figure 2

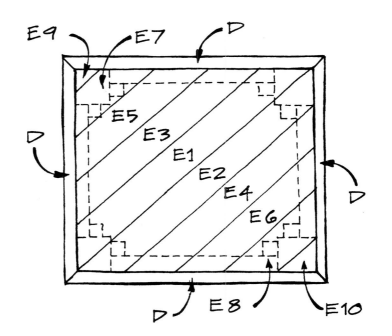

Figure 3

OUTDOOR TABLE/SEAT

After completing our new patio table (see the previous project), I planned to build four seats to go with it. However, now that we have them, we use them not only as seats, but as outdoor cocktail tables and ottomans. We also place them side by side and use them as a bench. They are very easy to build, and the cost is next to nothing. These are made from treated pine, but you can also use redwood. Just be sure to use waterproof wood glue during the construction.

MATERIALS LIST

Lumber:

11 linear ft. 2 x 4 treated lumber
8 linear ft. 1 x 4 treated lumber

Hardware:

approx. 20 #6 x 1-1/2" galvanized flathead wood screws
approx. 25 #10 x 3-1/2" galvanized flathead wood screws

CUTTING LIST

Code	Description	Qty.	Material	Dimensions
A	Leg	4	2 x 4 treated lumber	18" long
B	Leg Support	4	2 x 4 treated lumber	10" long
C	Center Support	1	2 x 4 treated lumber	13" long
D	Slat	5	1 x 4 treated lumber	17" long

Constructing the Sides

1. Cut four legs (A) from 2 x 4 treated lumber, each 18 inches long.

2. Cut four leg supports (B) from 2 x 4 treated lumber, each 10 inches long.

3. Assemble one side as shown in *Figure 1*, placing two leg supports (B) between two legs (A). One leg support (B) should be flush with the ends of the two legs (A), and the second leg support (B) should be placed 4 inches from the opposite ends of the legs (A). Glue and screw the assembly together, using 3-1/2-inch-long screws. Use two screws for each joint. Drive the screws at an angle (toenail) through the top and bottom edges of each leg support (B) into each leg (A). Repeat this process to assemble the second side.

4. Cut one 13-inch-long center support (C) from 2 x 4 treated lumber.

5. Perform this next assembly on a level work surface to make certain that the finished base is level. Place the center support (C) between the two sides, as shown in *Figure 2*, and screw it in place using 3-1/2-inch screws. Drive the screws through the face of each leg support (B) into the ends of the center support (C).

Figure 1

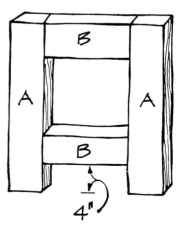

117

Figure 2

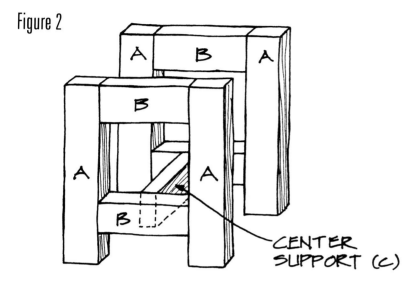

CENTER SUPPORT (C)

Adding the Slats

1. Cut five slats (D) from 1 x 4 treated lumber, each 17 inches long.

2. Place the five slats (D) side by side on top of the base assembly *(Figure 3)*, with their cut ends facing the sides. They should overhang the base on all four sides by about 1/2 inch. Secure the four slats by screwing them to the base assembly using 1-1/2-inch-long screws. (TIP: It looks much nicer if you draw a line on the slats from the front of the base to the back, about 1 inch from the slat ends, and place all of your screws on that line.) Put two screws on each end of each slat, and space them uniformly on all slats.

Finishing

1. Sand the completed project carefully (people will be sitting on this!).

2. Using exterior-grade materials, stain or paint the finished table/ seat the color of your choice.

Figure 3

C

MATERIALS LIST

Lumber:

18 linear ft. 2 x 4 treated lumber
16 linear ft. 2 x 6 treated lumber
15 linear ft. 1 x 4 treated lumber
11 linear ft. 2 x 4 treated lumber (optional)

Hardware:

approx. 50 #6 x 1-1/2" galvanized flathead wood screws
approx. 75 #10 x 3-1/2" galvanized flathead wood screws

Special Tools and Techniques:

miters

CUTTING LIST

Code	Description	Qty.	Material	Dimensions
A	Armrest	2	2 x 4 treated lumber	21" long
B	Leg	4	2 x 4 treated lumber	25" long
C	Side Support	4	2 x 4 treated lumber	18" long
D	Trim	10	1 x 4 treated lumber	17" long
E	Seat	3	2 x 6 treated lumber	60" long

PATIO BENCH

This patio bench provides seating for three people—or for four dearest and closest friends—yet it doesn't take up much space on your deck or patio. It is relatively inexpensive to make, and the construction is a snap. The finished bench dimensions are 67 inches wide and 21 inches deep.

Making the Side Panels

The side panels are constructed from 2 x 4s and trimmed with 1 x 4s on the outside.

1. From the 2 x 4 treated lumber, cut one 21-inch-long armrest (A), two legs (B), each 25 inches long, and two side supports (C), each 18 inches long.

2. With the armrest (A) standing on edge, miter both ends at a 45-degree angle as shown in *Figure 1*.

3. In the same manner, miter one end of both legs (B) at a 45-degree angle.

4. Attach the armrest (A) to the two legs (B) and two side supports (C) to form the side assembly illustrated in *Figure 1*. Note that the lower side support (C) is positioned 8 inches from the bottom of the legs (B), and the upper side support is positioned 7-1/2 inches from the lower edge of the armrest (A). Screw the pieces together using two 3-1/2-inch-long screws to secure each joint.

5. Repeat Steps 1 through 4 to make the second side.

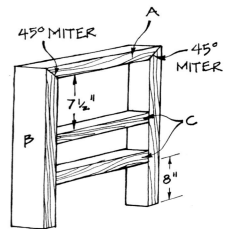

Figure 1

119

PATIO
BENCH

Adding the Trim

1. Cut five trim pieces (D) from 1 x 4 treated lumber, each 17 inches long. They are attached to the outer edges of the bench side panels.

2. Place the five trim pieces (D) side by side on top of the side panels *(Figure 2)*. The outermost trim pieces (D) should be flush with the outer edges of the legs (A), and the remaining three trim pieces (D) should be evenly spaced in the middle.

3. Secure the five trim pieces by screwing them to the armrest (A) and to the side supports using 1-1/2-inch-long screws. Space the screws uniformly, and use two screws for each end of all trim pieces. The finished bench looks much nicer if all of the screws are aligned across the trim pieces. To accomplish this, measure and mark 3/4 inch from both ends of each board, draw lines across each trim piece at the marks, and put all of your screws on those lines.

Adding the Bench Seat

1. Cut three seat pieces (E) from 2 x 6 treated lumber, each 60 inches long.

2. Position the side assemblies with the trim (D) facing out, and attach the seat pieces (E) to the upper side supports (C), as shown in *Figure 3*. Use three 3-1/2-inch-long screws at each end of each seat piece (E).

3. An optional step (if your bench will be subjected to lots of weight) is to attach two 2 x 4 braces, each 60 inches long, to the lower side supports (C).

Finishing

1. Sand the completed project very carefully.

2. Stain or paint the finished bench the color of your choice using exterior-grade materials.

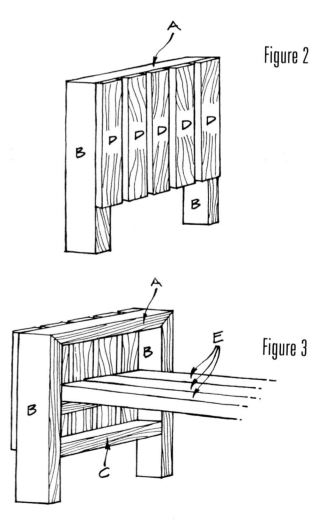

Figure 2

Figure 3

This patio chair is a real success story. Not only is it extremely inexpensive to make, but it's good-looking and incredibly comfortable. This one is made from pressure-treated 2 x 4 and 1 x 6 lumber, but you could also make it using redwood. Use waterproof glue if you plan to leave the finished chair exposed to the elements.

MATERIALS LIST

Lumber:

24 linear ft. 2 x 4 treated lumber
12 linear ft. 1 x 6 treated lumber

Hardware:

approx. 50 #6 x 1-1/4" galvanized flathead wood screws
approx. 10 #8 x 2-1/2" galvanized flathead wood screws
approx. 25 #12 x 4-1/2" galvanized flathead wood screws

Special Tools and Techniques:

miters
bevels

PATIO CHAIR

CUTTING LIST

Code	Description	Qty.	Material	Dimensions
A	Arm	2	2 x 4 treated lumber	21" long
B	Leg	4	2 x 4 treated lumber	28" long
C	Side Support	2	2 x 4 treated lumber	14" long
D	Seat Front	1	2 x 4 treated lumber	18-1/2" long
E	Seat Side	2	2 x 4 treated lumber	19-1/2" long
F	Seat Back	1	2 x 4 treated lumber	15-1/2" long
G	Slat	4	1 x 6 treated lumber	18-1/2" long
H	Back Support	2	2 x 4 treated lumber	14-1/2" long
I	Back Slat	3	1 x 6 treated lumber	18-1/2" long

Constructing the Sides

1. From 2 x 4 treated lumber, cut one 21-inch-long chair arm (A), two chair legs (B), each 28 inches long, and one 14-inch-long side support (C).

2. Setting the chair arm (A) on its face, miter both ends at a 45-degree angle as shown in *Figure 1.*

3. Setting each chair leg (B) on its face, miter just one end at a 45-degree angle (also shown in *Figure 1*).

4. To assemble one chair side, place the side support (C) between the chair legs (B), and the chair arm (A) between the two mitered ends of the two chair legs (B). (This is illustrated in *Figure 1*). Glue and screw them in place using one 4-1/2-inch-long screw for each end of the arm, screwing through the edge of the chair arm (A) into the mitered end of the adjacent chair leg (B). Then, with another 4-1/2-inch-long screw for each leg, screw through the edge of the chair leg (B) into the mitered end of the chair arm (A).

Figure 1

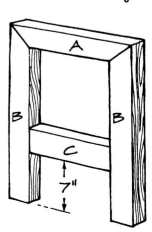

5. Repeat Steps 1 through 4 to assemble a second chair side.

Constructing the Seat

1. From 2 x 4 treated lumber, cut one 18-1/2-inch-long seat front (D), two seat sides (E), each 19-1/2 inches long, and one 15-1/2-inch-long seat back (F).

2. Assemble the seat according to the illustration in *Figure 2*. Use two 2-1/2-inch-long screws on each end of the overlapping boards. Note that the front (D) extends over the ends of the sides (E), and the back (F) fits between the sides (E).

Figure 2

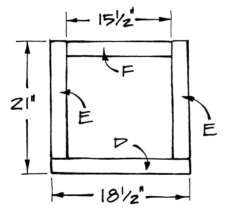

3. As shown in *Figure 3*, attach the assembled seat between the two chair sides 14-1/2 inches from the bottom ends of the chair legs (B). Use two 4-1/2-inch-long screws driven through the face of each leg to secure the seat.

4. Cut four slats (G) from 1 x 6 treated lumber, each 18-1/2 inches long. Place them side by side on top of the seat assembly, with their ends facing the chair sides *(see Figure 4)*. The slats should overhang both the front and back of the chair by about 1/2 inch. Secure the four slats by gluing and screwing them to the seat assembly with 1-1/4-inch-long screws. (TIP: It looks much nicer if you draw a line on the slats from the front of the chair to the back— about 1 inch from the slat ends— and place all of your screws on that line.) Put two screws on each end of a slat, and space them uniformly on all of the slats.

Adding the Chair Back

1. Cut two back supports (H) from 2 x 4 treated lumber, each 14-1/2 inches long. Then set your saw blade to cut 15 degrees off vertical, and bevel one end of each support to allow the assembled back to lean slightly backwards. (If you're unsure about how to make a bevel cut, refer to the "Tips and Techniques" chapter.)

2. Cut three back slats (I) from 1 x 6 treated lumber, each 18-1/2 inches long.

3. Assemble the chair back by attaching the three back slats (I) to the two back supports (H). The ends of the back slats (I) should be flush with the faces of the two back supports (H). As shown in *Figure 4*, the slats should be flush at the beveled end and extend approximately 1-1/2 inches over the other end of the back support (H). Again, draw a line to guide your screw placement, and use two 1-1/4-inch-long screws on each end of each slat.

4. Fit the assembled back between the chair sides so that the beveled ends of the back supports (H) rest on the rear chair slat (G). Attach the back to the chair by screwing through the chair sides into the back support (H). Use two or three 4-1/2-inch-long screws through each side.

Finishing

1. Sand the completed chair carefully (splinters on a chair can prove to be most uncomfortable).

2. Stain or paint the chair the color of your choice using exterior-grade finishing materials.

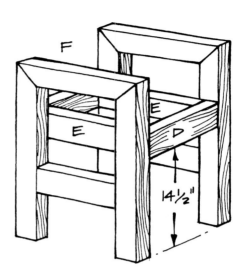

Figure 3

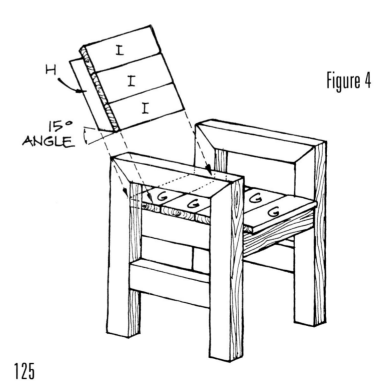

Figure 4

My caladiums have been a lot happier since they found a
new home in this patio planter. I placed it outside my din-
ing room window so that we can enjoy our plants whether
we are inside or outside. This project is perfect for using
scrap lumber from other outdoor projects. I used leftover
1 x 6 treated lumber from building our deck. Be sure to
use waterproof glue for all assemblies.

MATERIALS LIST

Lumber:

22 linear ft. 1 x 4 rough cedar
26 linear ft. 1 x 6 treated lumber
19 linear ft. 2 x 4 treated lumber
1 pc. exterior-grade plywood, 11" x 48"

Hardware:

approx. 50 #6 x 2" galvanized flathead wood screws
approx. 100 #6 x 2-1/2" galvanized flathead wood screws
approx. 100 #10 x 3-1/2" galvanized flathead wood screws
approx. 50 8d galvanized finishing nails

Special Tools and Techniques:

miters

PATIO PLANTER

CUTTING LIST

Code	Description	Qty.	Material	Dimensions
A	Vertical	22	1 x 6 treated lumber	14" long
B	Horizontal Support	4	2 x 4 treated lumber	48" long
C	Side Support	4	2 x 4 treated lumber	7" long
D	Bottom	1	exterior-grade plywood	11" x 48"
E	Short Trim	2	1 x 4 rough cedar	12-1/2" long
F	Long Trim	2	1 x 4 rough cedar	51" long
G	Long Frame	2	1 x 4 rough cedar	51" long
H	Short Frame	2	1 x 4 rough cedar	14" long

Building the Front and Back

1. Cut eighteen vertical pieces (A) from 1 x 6 treated lumber, each 14 inches long.

2. Cut four horizontal support pieces (B) from 2 x 4 treated lumber, each 48 inches long.

3. Place nine vertical pieces (A) side by side on a level surface. As illustrated in *Figure 1*, position one horizontal support piece (B) so that it is even with the ends of the vertical pieces (A) and centered over the width of the nine boards. Note that the vertical pieces (A) extend 3/4 inch beyond each end of the horizontal support (B). Place a second horizontal support piece (B) 1 inch from the opposite ends of the vertical pieces (A), again centered over the width of the nine boards (*Figure 1*).

Figure 1

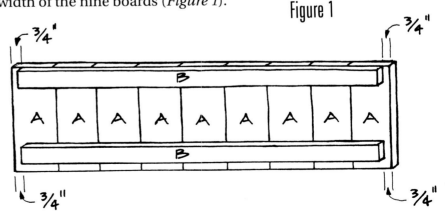

127

4. After you are certain of their position, attach both of the horizontal support pieces (B) to the nine vertical pieces (A) using exterior glue and 3-1/2-inch-long galvanized screws. Use at least two screws for each of the vertical pieces (A).

5. Repeat Steps 3 and 4. You have now constructed both the front and back sections.

Building the Sides

To build the side sections, follow the same procedure that you used for the front and back. The only difference is that the sides are narrower.

1. Cut four vertical pieces (A) from 1 x 6 treated lumber, each 14 inches long.

2. Cut four side support pieces (C) from 2 x 4 treated lumber, each 7 inches long.

3. Place two vertical pieces (A) side by side on a level surface. Center one support piece (C) over the width of the two boards and position it flush with the ends of the vertical pieces (A). Note that the vertical pieces (A) extend 1-1/2 inches on each end of the side supports (C). Place a second support piece (C) 1 inch from the opposite ends of the vertical pieces (A). Again, center it over the width of the two boards. (Refer to *Figure 1*.)

4. Attach both support pieces (C) to the two vertical pieces (A) using exterior glue and 3-1/2-inch-long galvanized screws. Use at least two screws on each of the vertical pieces (A).

5. Repeat Steps 3 and 4. You have now constructed both of the side sections.

Assembling the Planter

1. Cut one 11-inch by 48-inch bottom piece (D) from exterior grade plywood.

2. This is one of those times when you probably need a willing helper (or sixteen of your own hands). You now have a long front section, a long back section, and two short side sections. Each of the sections has two attached support pieces: one that is flush with the edges, and one that is offset by 1 inch. The flush supports belong at the top of the assembled planter, and the offset supports brace the plywood bottom.

Place the two assembled side sections between the front and back sections, fitting the plywood bottom (D) over the lower supports as shown in *Figure 2*. Note that the vertical pieces (A) on the front and back sections overlap the edges of the vertical pieces (A) on the side sections.

Figure 2

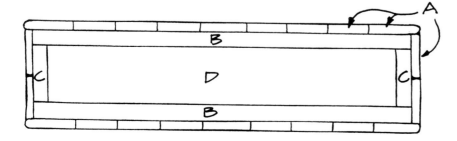

3. Glue and screw the sections together on the ends, using several 3-1/2-inch-long screws on each corner to make certain that the assembly is secure. Then glue and screw the plywood bottom (D) to the lower supports all the way around the planter. Use the 2-inch-long screws for this assembly, placing one about every six inches.

4. Now take a break. That last step was a killer.

Adding the Trim

1. Cut two short trim pieces (E) from 1 x 4 rough cedar, each 12-1/2 inches long.

2. Cut two long trim pieces (F) from 1 x 4 rough cedar, each 51 inches long.

3. Attach the short trim pieces (E) flush with the top of the planter side sections, overlapping the ends of the front and back sections, as shown in *Figure 3*. Use exterior glue and 2-1/2-inch-long screws, inserting at least two screws into each vertical (A).

4. Again using exterior glue and at least two 2-1/2-inch-long screws for each vertical (A), attach the long trim pieces (F) flush with the top of the planter front and back sections. Overlap the ends of the short trim pieces (E) as shown in *Figure 3*.

5. The final step adds a mitered frame to cover all of the exposed edges of the planter top. Cut two

long frame pieces (G) from 1 x 4 rough cedar, each 51 inches long.

6. Cut two short frame pieces (H) from 1 x 4 rough cedar, each 14 inches long.

7. Setting each piece on its face, miter both ends of each of the frame pieces (G and H) at a 45-degree angle. The outer edges of the frame should just cover the previously attached trim pieces (E and F).

8. Attach the four frame pieces (G and H) to the top of the planter using exterior wood glue and 8-penny galvanized finishing nails spaced about 6 inches apart.

Finishing

1. Lightly sand the entire planter to remove large splinters.

2. The finished project should be sealed with an exterior wood finish. I used a maple stain followed by a clear wood sealer, but you can stain it the color of your choice.

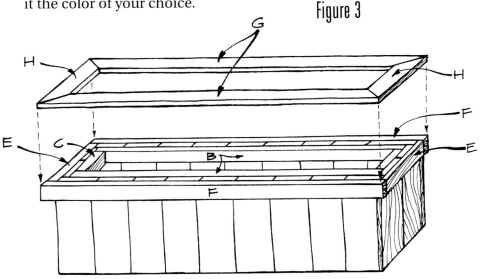

Figure 3

RAISED-PANEL PLANTER

This planter box has raised panels on each of the four sides. It's a beautiful display container for any plant, and it's easier to make than you might suppose. If you plan to use your planter outside, be sure to purchase exterior-grade materials, including lumber, hardware, glue, and finishes. I made this one mainly for indoor use (I bring it outside to use as a decoration for the deck when we have parties), so I used pine and stained it. The completed planter is 12 inches square and 12 inches tall; it will perfectly accommodate a 10-inch pot.

MATERIALS LIST

Lumber:

5 linear ft. 1 x 12 pine
17 linear ft. 1 x 4 pine

Hardware:

approx. 50 3d finishing nails

Special Tools and Techniques:

bevels
dadoes
miters

CUTTING LIST

Code	Description	Qty.	Material	Dimensions
A	Panel	4	1 x 12 pine	8-5/8" x 8-5/8"
B	Frame	16	1 x 4 pine, ripped	12" long
C	Bottom	1	1 x 12 pine	10-1/2" x 10-1/2"

Making the Sides

The four planter sides are all constructed identically. Although they look very professional, raised-panel sides are not difficult to do. Just take your time and make sure that all of the pieces have the correct dimensions. Each side consists of a beveled panel that is fitted into an outer frame.

1. Cut one 8-5/8-inch-square panel (A) from 1 x 12 pine.

2. Set your saw blade to cut 15 degrees off vertical, and make a 2-inch-long bevel on all four edges of the panel (A). The remaining thickness of the cut edge of the panel should be 1/8 inch. A diagram of the resulting cut is shown in *Figure 1*.

3. Rip a total of 4-plus linear feet of 1 x 4 pine to a width of 2 inches. (You need a little more than 4 feet to allow for the material lost with each saw cut.)

4. Cut four frame pieces (B) from the ripped 1 x 4 pine, each 12 inches long.

5. Setting each frame piece (B) on its 2-inch face, miter both ends at a 45-degree angle.

6. The panel (A) floats in dadoes that are cut into the inside edges of all four frame pieces. Cut a dado 1/4 inch wide and 3/8 inch deep into the shorter edge of each frame piece (B). See *Figure 2*. (For some assistance in cutting dadoes, refer to the "Tips and Techniques" section.)

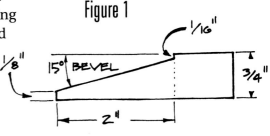

Figure 1

7. The side should first be assembled without glue or nails, to make certain that all of the pieces fit perfectly. First place the panel (A) and four side frames (B) on a level surface. Then, referring to *Figure 2*, fit the panel (A) into the dadoes in the frame pieces (B).

8. When you are satisfied that all of the pieces fit correctly, glue and clamp the frame together and let it sit for a few hours. Do not glue the panel (A) in the dadoes—it should float there.

9. Repeat steps 2 through 8 three more times to make the remaining planter sides.

Figure 2

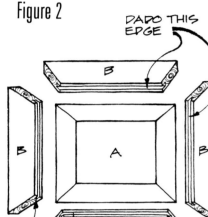

Assembling the Planter

1. In order to fit together properly, the four assembled sides must be beveled on two opposing edges, as shown in *Figure 3*. Set your saw blade to cut 45 degrees off vertical, and bevel two opposing edges on each of the four assembled sides. Note that the bevels on each side are mirror images of each other.

2. Cut one 10-1/2-inch-square bottom (C) from 1 x 12 pine.

3. Place the bottom (C) on a level surface. Then fit the four paneled sides around the bottom (C), matching the beveled edges. Glue and clamp the assembly together, and let the glue set up for a couple of hours.

4. To reinforce the joints you have just glued, drive 3-penny finishing nails through the face of each side into the beveled edge of the adjoining side. Use about three nails for each joint. Also drive nails through the lower face of each paneled side into the edge of the bottom (C). Again use about three nails on each side. Countersink all of the nails.

Finishing

1. Fill any exposed nail holes with wood filler.

2. Sand the completed planter.

3. Stain or paint the finished planter the color of your choice. I used a dark cherry stain.

Figure 3

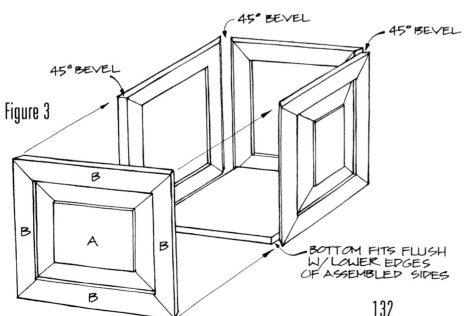

MATERIALS LIST

Lumber:

1 pc. 3/4" exterior-grade plywood, 15" x 25"
18 linear ft. 2 x 8 treated lumber
5 linear ft. 3-1/2" decorative trim

Hardware:

approx. 20 #6 x 2-1/2" galvanized flathead wood screws
approx. 20 2d galvanized finishing nails
approx. 100 6d galvanized finishing nails
approx. 20 8d galvanized finishing nails
brass sundial, approx. 10-1/2" dia.
approx. 16 brass upholstery tacks

Special Tools and Techniques:

bevels
miters

SUNDIAL

CUTTING LIST

Code	Description	Qty.	Material	Dimensions
A	Top	1	3/4" exterior-grade plywood	see *Fig. 1* (approx. 13" x 15")
B	Inner Support	1	3/4" exterior-grade plywood	see *Fig. 2* (approx. 10" x 11")
C	Column Side	6	2 x 8 treated lumber	35" long
D	Trim	6	3-1/2" decorative trim	cut to fit (approx. 54" total)

Getting the Parts Ready

1. A pattern for the top (A) is given in *Figure 1*. The top (A) is a hexagon with all sides measuring exactly 7-1/2 inches, and all angles measuring 60 degrees. Enlarge the pattern and cut one top (A) from 3/4-inch-thick plywood.

2. *Figure 2* shows the pattern for the inner support (B). It is a smaller hexagon, and all of its sides mea-sure 5-1/2 inches. Enlarge the pat-tern and cut one inner support (B) from 3/4-inch-thick plywood.

3. Cut six column sides (C) from 2 x 8 treated lumber, each 35 inches long.

4. Set your saw blade to cut 30 degrees off vertical, and bevel both 35-inch-long edges of all six column sides. The resulting angle on each edge of the wood is 60 degrees, as shown in *Figure 3*. Note that the

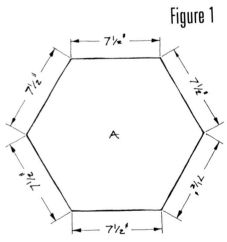

Figure 1

(Enlarge by 800% to get actual size.)

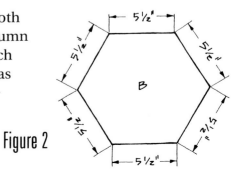

Figure 2

133

SUNDIAL

Although I still haven't thrown away my watch, and hardly ever run to the garden to see what time it is, it's still fun to have this sundial in my yard. I painted mine a bright red, but you can choose another color or simply stain it.

The column is easy to build out of exterior-grade plywood and 2 x 8 treated lumber (I used pressure-treated pine). Be sure to use only exterior-grade materials, including your lumber, fasteners, adhesive, and finish. You can find the brass fixture, the sundial itself, at most garden shops and building supply stores. The finished sundial is approximately 16 inches in diameter and about 36 inches tall.

bevels are mirror images of each other.

Assembling the Column

This assembly is simple to do, but there are lots of parts to handle at one time. You may wish to enlist the assistance of a willing helper.

1. The first step is to attach one end of all six column sides (C) to the top (A). Stand the column sides on end so that they form a circle. As shown in *Figure 4*, the narrower face of each column side (C) is oriented toward the inside of the circle.

2. Place the top (A) onto the upper ends of the column sides (C). Make certain that the edges of the top (A) are flush with the outer faces of the column sides (C). Using glue and 2-1/2-inch-long screws, attach the top to the column sides. Drive two screws through the top (A) into the end of each column side (C). Countersink the screws.

3. Turn the column upside down, and fit the inner support (B) inside the circle formed by the column sides (C). Position the inner support (B) about 4 inches from the ends of the column sides.

4. Glue and nail the inner support (B) in place. Use 8-penny finishing nails and drive two nails through each of the column sides (C) into the edges of the inner support (B). Countersink the nails.

5. Use 6-penny nails to reinforce each of the joints between the column sides. Nail through the beveled edge of one column side (C) into the beveled edge of the adjoining column side (C), spacing the nails about 6 inches apart down the length of the joint. Countersink the nails.

Adding the Trim

1. Carefully measure and cut six pieces of 3-1/2-inch-wide decorative trim (D) to fit around the top of the column. It is easier if you cut one piece at a time and give yourself a little extra length for cutting the miters. Standing the trim pieces (D) on edge, miter both ends of each piece. Set your saw to cut at 30 degrees, producing an angle of 60 degrees on the wood. These miters match the bevels in the column sides.

2. Glue and nail the decorative trim pieces (D) on each side of the column, positioning the pieces so that the thicker edges are flush with the top (A). Use two 2-penny finishing nails to secure each of the trim pieces (D).

Finishing

1. Fill any exposed nail and screw holes with wood filler.

2. Sand the completed column.

3. Stain or paint the finished column the color of your choice using exterior-grade materials.

4. Center the brass sundial on top of the column, and use about 16 brass upholstery tacks spaced evenly around the sundial to hold it in place.

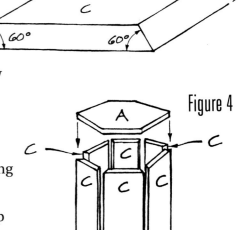

Figure 3

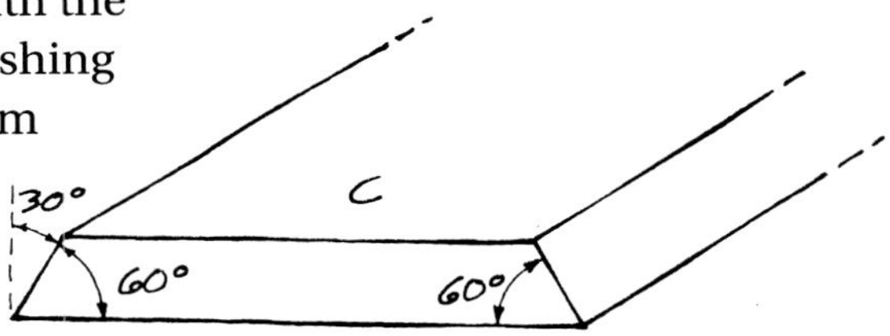

Figure 4

Index

Acknowledgements

One of the special joys of writing a book is the joy of working with so many special people who contribute their time, their caring, and their expertise. For their unique talents and invaluable assistance, I am grateful.

To Mark Baldwin, master craftsperson, who contributed his design ideas and his considerable woodworking expertise. I admire your skills and would have been lost without your efforts.

To Preston Poe, who assisted in the photography and schlepped furniture for days. Thanks for your creative talent, for always being there for me, and for your caring.

To my publisher, Rob Pulleyn, who sets the standard for the industry. Would that every writer could be so lucky! Thanks for your professionalism and your never-failing sense of humor.

To Evan Bracken, who photographed the projects and made it look so easy, and who kept all of us going during the shoot.

To my editor, Leslie Dierks, who cared about this book and made it so much better.

To my dear friends, Pat Connolly and Jane Hamada, who got me into this.

Lastly and most importantly, to my incredible husband, Jim, for his encouragement, his insight, his patience, and his remarkable wit. I love you.

Thanks go to GarrettWade Company for providing the photographs on pages 7, 17, 20 and 21, and to Westall & Johnson Chandley Lumber Company for making their yard available.